rock and
water plants

PRACTICAL GARDENING HANDBOOK

rock and water plants

PETER ROBINSON

with photography by peter anderson

LORENZ BOOKS

This edition is published by Lorenz Books

Lorenz Books is an imprint of Anness Publishing Ltd
Hermes House, 88–89 Blackfriars Road
London SE1 8HA
tel. 020 7401 2077; fax 020 7633 9499
www.lorenzbooks.com; info@anness.com

© Anness Publishing Ltd 2003, 2004

UK agent: The Manning Partnership Ltd,
6 The Old Dairy, Melcombe Road, Bath BA2 3LR;
tel. 01225 478444; fax 01225 478440;
sales@manning-partnership.co.uk

UK distributor: Grantham Book Services Ltd,
Isaac Newton Way, Alma Park Industrial Estate,
Grantham, Lincs NG31 9SD;
tel. 01476 541080; fax 01476 541061;
orders@gbs.tbs-ltd.co.uk

North American agent/distributor:
National Book Network,
4501 Forbes Boulevard, Suite 200,
Lanham, MD 20706;
tel. 301 459 3366; fax 301 429 5746;
www.nbnbooks.com

Australian agent/distributor:
Pan Macmillan Australia,
Level 18, St Martins Tower, 31 Market St,
Sydney, NSW 2000;
tel. 1300 135 113; fax 1300 135 103;
customer.service@macmillan.com.au

New Zealand agent/distributor: David Bateman Ltd,
30 Tarndale Grove, Off Bush Road,
Albany, Auckland;
tel. (09) 415 7664; fax (09) 415 8892

A CIP catalogue record for this book is available from
the British Library.

Publisher: Joanna Lorenz
Managing Editor: Judith Simons
Executive Editor: Caroline Davison
Designer: Kathryn Gammon
Editorial Reader: Jan Cutler
Production Controller: Wendy Lawson

Previously published as part of a larger volume,
Rock and Water Gardening.

1 2 3 4 5 6 7 8 9 10

Note: It is important to ask a qualified electrician to install
any outside power supply. The publishers cannot be held
responsible for any accident or injury that may occur as a
result of using this book.

C O N T E N T S

There is a strong affinity between rock and water, and creating a successful partnership between these

INTRODUCTION

two elements is one of the most challenging, but rewarding, tasks in garden design and construction. Rock and water have been used in gardens by various cultures, and these features can be recreated in every type of space, from small city rooftops to large country gardens.

OPPOSITE: **A seat in an informal garden provides the perfect vantage point from which to view this delightful pool.**

WHY ROCK AND WATER?

OPPOSITE: **Lush, exotic-looking planting along the edge of a cascading watercourse can create an enticingly tropical effect.**

BELOW: **Making a watercourse with slate is one of the most creative challenges in water gardening. Note how the angular strata of the slate pieces are parallel.**

Dig a hole in your garden and you begin a process that can change your life. Make the hole watertight, add water and you have a pool. Shape the excavated soil and use your imagination to add rocks, and a rocky water feature evolves. Add plants, and a water garden is born. As soon as you decide to break away from the stereotype of a pool circumscribed by irregular paving or evenly shaped paving slabs, there are unparalleled opportunities to be creative with natural materials.

THE APPEAL OF ROCK AND WATER

Working with rock and water is an artistic process that does not lend itself to the quick-fix, self-assembly package. An artist knows how important it is to spend time on establishing the initial framework; artists do not take shortcuts or scrimp on costs at this stage. Simplicity is one of the keys to success in a good design, and boldness in the initial design is important. For this reason, explore all possible options in natural materials and be confident with your initial outline. This may mean that a large part of your budget is used

on equipment that allows you to use larger stones. Even apparently inaccessible sites can have large rocks slung in by a road crane, and a small cultivator can be lifted in at the same time to help with excavating and positioning. There are few schemes in which including a few large rocks will not have more impact than using a greater number of smaller rocks, all the same size and shape, and it is not true that larger pieces are appropriate only in large gardens: one large piece of rock in or near a pool in a small courtyard can have great impact.

No matter how small the size of the water feature, it is important to think about the selection of each rock, how it is presented to its neighbours, the way the faces are positioned, how deeply it is buried and which side is uppermost. If you do not take this trouble, the beauty of each individual rock may not be seen, and a substantial combination of pieces will quickly look unco-ordinated and unnatural. For this reason a gardener may be deterred from attempting a scheme that combines rock and water in favour of a water feature that can be placed in the hands of a landscape contractor or built on a do-it-yourself basis, where the skills required may seem less daunting. The rewards resulting from creating a successful water and rock garden are so great, however, that they more than outweigh any problems that the process may present.

The main essentials to creating a rock and water feature are having an appreciation of the natural landscape and, at a practical level, having some help in lifting the rocks if they are large. Every natural rock pool, stream, river or pool has its own beauty, and each person will interpret these features in a different way. Ideally, the scheme should carry the imprint of your own character, so there is much to be said for playing a direct part in its design. Once the rocks are in position and the water feature is established, it takes a brave person to dismantle the scheme to make adjustments.

It is essential, therefore, that the initial placing is right and that you do not rely on planting to disguise weaknesses. If you are happy with the skeleton of the scheme before any plants are used, you will be doubly satisfied when the plants begin to become established and clothe the rocks.

There is now a greater range of materials and plants available than ever before and nowhere is this variety more apparent than in the availability of natural rocks

and materials for building and refining a water feature. Because of the cost of transportation, the choice of rock used to be determined by the proximity of quarries. Now, most good garden centres offer a good range of rock-garden stone and cobbles, and you can select individual rock pieces for even size and weight. You will find an even better selection of rocks if you are prepared to visit specialist suppliers. Because the rocks are likely to have the greatest influence on the overall character of a water garden, choosing individual rocks can be one of the most exciting parts of the early planning.

Given the importance and long-term impact that the choice and size of rock will have, make this a key decision and allocate it the lion's share of the budget. It

is comparatively easy to relocate or replace plants if you are unhappy with their position after the planting has settled in. Moving or changing a rock is not easy, and it is better to postpone a scheme altogether rather than choose the bones of your water garden too hastily.

A well-made water garden is a joy and will give increasing pleasure as the scheme becomes established. Plants can be added, changed, pruned or thinned. Bogs or beds for moisture-lovers can be added, and areas of marginal planting can be established. Specimen trees can be planted to add winter reflection. The planting is, in a sense, the icing on the cake, and it should be the final task that brings the scheme alive.

INFLUENCE OF THE ORIENT

The Chinese and, later, the Japanese were masters of the art of using water and rock. The Chinese garden was strongly linked to the poetic and artistic ethos, and their religion taught the Chinese to revere nature and to regard the garden as a bond with it. The most powerful symbols of nature were mountains and lakes, and this natural contrast was reflected in the garden through the use of rock and water. This contrast echoed the Taoist principle of yin and yang, the unity of opposites, and even in smaller courtyard gardens, a large rock would be included to represent a mountain beside a small pool.

The rocks selected were usually weatherworn limestones, sometimes with quite grotesque shapes, that were dredged out from the bottom of lakes. The rough, towering mountains were more easily represented by the use of eroded rocks, and the holes worn in the rocks over time allowed the light and shadow in the crevices to have maximum effect as a picture. A single rock was used in much the same way as a large statue in Western gardens, and it would be carefully positioned so that it could be admired from every side.

From the Chinese garden sprang the Japanese style, which was greatly influenced by priests returning from China after studying Zen Buddhism. The Japanese shared with the Chinese a veneration for nature, but they refined their gardens with a greater use of symbolism and resorted to the strict placement of ornaments and planting. Unlike the Chinese garden, which was planned as a series of pictures, the Japanese garden was made into one complete whole, with one of a series of disciplined styles predominating.

Instead of copying nature in their gardens, the Japanese strove to capture its essence. Water and rock were equally important, with islands and pools

BELOW: **Rigid** attention to the choice and placing of hard landscape features is a feature of oriental gardens. The *shishi-odoshi* or Japanese deer scarer provides added interest with its sound and movement.

fed by waterfalls or water rushing through rocks. Waterfalls were greatly admired, and many large landscape gardens were dominated by a carefully sited waterfall. Such features were generally located away from the main house, falling from a valley between two mountains with a background of dense forest. Where there was no water available, a rocky bed would be created to give the appearance of a dried river bed and to represent water.

The symbolism employed in the placing of stones, lanterns and bridges, so important and obvious to the trained Japanese eye, was lost to all but a few gardeners from the West. But even though their significance was not always understood, this did not prevent these gardens from being greatly admired.

OTHER INFLUENCES

Although it might be argued that the oriental influence has had the greatest impact on the use of rock and water in modern garden design, earlier influences from Islam had an equally strong impact on the formal use of water. Early Islamic gardens provided relief and refreshment from the searing heat. Water was formed into long, canal-like features, with nearby pathways and plants forming strict geometrical patterns. This influence spread to southern Spain. Indeed, one of the best-known examples of the use of canals and fountains can be seen at the fortress palace of Alhambra.

This refreshing use of formal water, so well perfected by the Islamic style, was further refined between the 15th and 18th centuries in northern India by the Mogul Emperors. Again there were the traditional canals in symmetrical patterns, but these Indian gardens particularly excelled in exploiting hillside situations to use the consequent water pressure for the most exhilarating fountains and spouts.

The romantic water garden, however, was perfected by the Romans who used water lavishly with statuary and ambitious planting. The gardens of the Renaissance, which centred on Rome, became famous for the noise and movement of water on a grand scale, and fountain design became an art form. Examples can be seen at the Villa d'Este, where ingenious design produced spouting dragons, water organs and the famous pathway of a hundred fountains.

In the latter part of the 15th century, the influence of the Italian Renaissance reached France and just over a century later it burst forth in the form of Le Nôtre's grand designs at Versailles. This set the scene across

Europe where Le Nôtre was imitated by the aristocracy of several countries. This extravagance in water garden design can still be seen in several country estates. Chatsworth, in Derbyshire, is a notable example.

In the mid-18th century, the break from the formal dominance of water in garden design came with a new informal movement in Britain. Compositions involving water used lakes, woodlands and bridges, and gradually the formal use of water receded to the immediate confines of the house. This became known as the Landscape Movement and its more naturalistic approach has had an increasing influence on our smaller gardens using rock and water.

TODAY'S GARDENS

In addition to the influences brought by various cultures to garden design, there is now a greater awareness of the environment than perhaps at any stage in our history and a greater sensitivity to the conservation of wildlife. Just as a reverence for nature was evident in the oriental tradition, the modern rock and water garden has a role to play in conservation. Most informal gardens attract wild creatures, but the combination of rock and water in an informal feature widens the diversity of visiting wildlife.

ABOVE: **This simple bridge, which disappears into vegetation on either side, provides a perfect crossing point. Leave gaps between the cross planks in order to allow the wood to expand when wet.**

The gardens in this chapter use rock and water in a variety of ways, and are designed to help you choose the

ROCK AND WATER IN GARDENS

best feature for your space. General examples of different rock and water features, such as pools and streams, are followed by a plan of a specific garden, which is accompanied by details on the choice of plants and on the important garden structures.

OPPOSITE: **The placement of rocks in this watercourse is superb and enhanced by the mix of plants.**

CHOOSING A STYLE

More and more homeowners are including water in their gardens. If you are planning to introduce water into your garden, it is important to choose a style that suits both your perception of a water garden and the existing features in the main garden. Although water will fit into any size or style of garden, it is particularly suitable for small gardens where the reflection of the sky in the water helps to relieve any feelings of claustrophobia which may be caused by high fences and walls.

When choosing from the many varieties of style it is possible to include, spend some time considering what you want water to do in your garden, and then spend even more time considering what form it should take.

RIGHT: **This water feature has a grey and yellow theme. The dark slate contrasts well with the edging of the yellow form of creeping Jenny** (*Lysimachia nummularia* 'Aurea').

OPPOSITE: **A gushing stream edged with rocks and flowers provides a perfect setting for relaxing.**

BELOW: **Here, a flat slab of the block-like rock pieces has been selected to act as the spillstone.**

DIFFERENT EFFECTS

The informal water garden will give absolute priority to blending into a natural style, where plants will dominate the overall picture. This style will suit the plantsperson, and offers considerable scope for introducing a lush type of planting which may not be possible in the remainder of the garden. The boundaries of this water garden may well extend into bog areas, and ample space to allow for this natural development should be considered whenever possible.

A formal pool is often the choice for a small garden where there is little or no lawn and the surface is dominated by paving. The formal pool has clearly defined

edges which are generally paved and form geometric shapes like squares, circles and rectangles. Planting is restrained, usually contained in aquatic planting crates and dominated by strong, upright leaves, such as those of irises, which will give a striking contrast to the horizontal expanse of water and the surrounding edges.

Raised pools are similar to formal pools in their suitability for a small space which is surrounded by paving. They are particularly suitable in courtyards or areas surrounded by high fences where they introduce reflected light. They make a good choice for the elderly or disabled as the water can be viewed and touched at close quarters. They are also a good choice if you wish to keep fish. Adding a fountain will also help the fish in heatwaves when oxygen levels are low at night.

Fountains introduce noise, movement and the sparkle of light. They are suitable for formal and informal settings, but are most appropriate in formal ones. Fountains are available in a variety of styles, from large tiered bowls, which spill water from bowl to bowl, to spouts which produce no more than a gentle gurgle in an urn. In addition to the many types of free-standing forms, there are also several informal styles that emerge from ground level through cobbles, millstones or rocks.

Streams and waterfalls bring magic to an informal garden. Even the most modest of slopes is suitable for a stream, and any large expanse of lawn may be relieved by streamside planting and the flow of water. Where there is sufficient gradient, a faster-moving rocky stream will enable you to grow a wider range of plants, such as alpines, in the dry soil near the edge. Creative gardeners will be in their element here with the chance to build waterfalls and rock pools, and fashion different sounds.

ROCK POOLS AND PONDS

The use of rock to form the edges of informal pools is one of the most creative design and construction techniques in water gardening. Every rock, no matter how small, contributes to the overall picture, requiring care in the individual positioning in relation to its neighbour and the other rocks used in the scheme, often extending well beyond the immediate surrounds of the pool. The aim is to create an air of natural informality, rather than an unnatural-looking ribbon of jagged rocks protruding from the surface of the water.

The choice of edge should be given very careful consideration at the planning stage. In small pools in sunny areas, the drop in level during the summer months should be anticipated, and an edge created which prevents an unsightly expanse of liner above the waterline. There is an extensive range of rock types that can be used, including limestone, slate, granite and sandstone. Washed boulders and cobbles have a natural affinity with water and are one of the simplest edges to construct, allowing water levels to vary with the season without exposing man-made liners.

ABOVE RIGHT: **The colour of this Welsh slate is enhanced when it is wet and surrounded by strong foliage colours.**

RIGHT: **An overuse of mortar in the making of retaining walls can soon be softened by covering them with prostrate plants such as broom and ivy.**

OPPOSITE: **In contrast to the angular and sloping formation of a slate watercourse, the strata of weatherworn limestone can be built to create almost horizontal lines.**

A SLATE ROCK POOL

This slate watercourse with its film of glistening water is constructed to run into a rock pool. The pool and rocks dominate a garden where interest is maintained in the winter months by conifers planted among the slate. The main viewing point across the wooden decking is from the living room of the house. The wooden decking overhangs the pool, which makes the watercourse appear to travel under the decking. Timber rounds hold back the soil mound, providing a sheltered niche for a shallow container planted with a delicate, cut-leaved Japanese maple (*Acer palmatum*). A "beach" of Caledonian cobbles links the decking to the rocks. The whole scene is framed with a timber pergola which is clothed in wisteria.

RIGHT: Decking tiles and a wisteria pergola form a superb frame for a slate watercourse.

INSET: The thin film of falling water absorbs large quantities of oxygen, which is a useful bonus for fish like orfe.

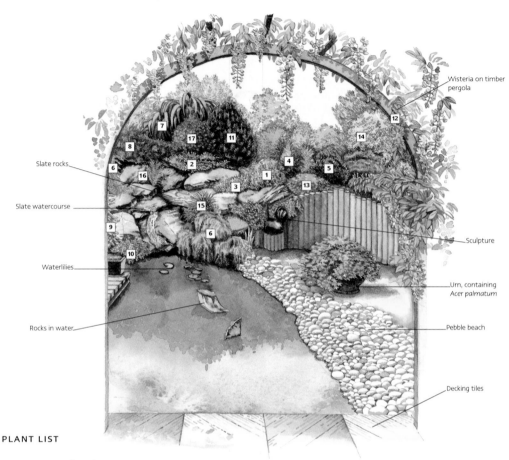

Wisteria on timber pergola

Slate rocks

Slate watercourse

Waterlilies

Rocks in water

Sculpture

Urn, containing
Acer palmatum

Pebble beach

Decking tiles

PLANT LIST

1 *Rosmarinus officinalis*
2 *Abies koreana* 'Silberlocke'
3 *Helianthemum* 'Rhodanthe Carneum'
4 *Pinus mugo* 'Mops'
5 *Pinus strobus* 'Radiata'
6 *Cedrus deodara* 'Golden Horizon'
7 *Phormium tenax* Purpureum Group
8 *Pinus sylvestris* 'Watereri'
9 *Abies procera* 'Glauca Prostrata'
10 *Cedrus deodara* 'Feelin' Blue'
11 *Pinus parviflora* 'Glauca'
12 *Wisteria sinensis*
13 *Tsuga canadensis* 'Jeddeloh'
14 *Pyrus salicifolia* 'Pendula'
15 *Acorus gramineus*
16 *Dryopteris filix-mas*
17 *Pinus heldreichii* var. *leucodermis*

USEFUL INFORMATION

MATERIALS
- Rock: 12 large pieces of slate for the main watercourse (total weight: 9,000kg/9 tons)
- Washed beach cobbles (1,000kg/1 ton)

PUMP SYSTEM
- Submersible pump under the decking (flow rate of 8,000 litres/2,113 gallons per hour)
- Ultra-violet clarifier under the decking (with two 9 watt u.v. bulbs) from which water is pumped to a biological filter via a 30mm (1¼in) corrugated hose
- Biological filter hidden behind conifers at the top of the watercourse (with three filtration chambers, brushes, profiled foam cartridges and biomedia)
- Spray bar for oxygenation installed above ground

POOL DIMENSIONS
- Area: 4.8 x 2.4m (16 x 8ft)
- Volume of 6,056 litres (1,600 gallons)

RAISED POOLS

Bringing the water surface nearer to eye level and so enhancing the tactile and visual delights of water is a frequently used design method. Whether to draw light into a tiny garden or to add coolness to a shady spot, the proximity of water is especially delightful when it takes the shape of a raised pool. Such pools are ideal in paved areas where a seat can be brought to the side of the pool and the paved surround used as an informal surface to place a refreshing drink. Reflection is a raised pool's particular asset, especially in small gardens with high walls or fences on their boundaries.

There need be no worry about digging holes and having to get rid of excavated soil. Furthermore, the often unforeseen hazards, such as pipework under the soil surface, which are often encountered during excavation, are not a problem with raised pools. If the outdoor space is small or is no more than a paved courtyard, then a raised pool is an excellent solution for incorporating water in the garden.

ABOVE: **In a sloping garden, a raised pool is given extra emphasis by a small, brick and decking surround, which is raised slightly higher than the pool.**

RIGHT: **This elegant raised pool is enhanced by the "peacock tail" effect of the cut sandstone walling pieces which are set into a recess in the wall above.**

LEFT: Railway sleepers make strong, stable edges for raised and partly raised pools.

LEFT: The horizontal lines of this raised brick surround are accentuated by the vertical lines of the planting, which includes iris, rushes and reedmaces.

A SHADY RAISED POOL

A cool, intimate sitting area surrounds this raised pool where the still, clear water forms the perfect foil for a mixed planting of ferns. Shade is provided by bamboo canes which form spokes from a central hub above the pool and radiate to a hexagon-shaped trellis that echoes the pool's outline. Extensive use has been made of variegated ivies to clothe the trellis and protect the pool from wind as well as to create privacy. To ease any feeling of claustrophobia, circular windows are cut in the trellis to form viewing points of features outside the area or to frame specimen plants in the windows. The shade is too heavy for waterlilies to flower well, but the water remains crystal clear and is broken by drifts of duckweed which are periodically netted off when they cover too much of the surface.

LEFT: **This hexagonal raised pool forms the centrepiece of a shady and sheltered garden retreat, which is surrounded by ivies and "moon windows" that are cut into the lath trellis-work.**

INSET: **The central walling blocks are built without mortar. The gaps between the blocks are then planted with ferns, which surround the column.**

Overhead bamboo canes

Trellis supporting *Hedera colchica* 'Sulphur Heart'

Raised pool

Seats

Fern tower (with mixed ferns) around bamboo pole

Hexagonal paving

PLANT LIST

1 *Hedera colchica*
  'Sulphur Heart'
2 *Acer palmatum* var. *dissectum*
  Dissectum Atropurpureum Group
  (grown in a container which is
  framed by a "moon" window)
3 A selection of mixed ferns, including
  Asplenium scolopendrium
  'Cristatum', *Blechnum spicant,
  Dryopteris erythrosora, D. sieboldii,
  Cystopteris dickieana* and
  Polypodium vulgare
4 *Lemna minor*
5 *Hosta fortunei* var. *aureomarginata*
6 *Hedera helix* 'Glacier'

USEFUL INFORMATION

MATERIALS
• Electric cable: buried under the
  surrounding paving and drawn
  through the twin walls of the raised
  pool to a switchbox on the outside of
  the twin wall (this allows a neat and
  hidden supply of electric power for any
  future pumps or lighting in the pool)
• A length of conduit: this is mortared
  just under the coping to allow cable to
  run from any electrical equipment
  inside the pool to the switchbox on the
  outside wall

CONSTRUCTION ADVICE
• Raised pools over 45cm (18in) high
  should be built with double walls on
  a 45cm- (18in-) wide foundation
  trench to withstand the pressure
  exerted by the water
• Wall ties set 1m (3ft) apart between
  the double walls provide extra strength
• The liner is fixed inside the inner
  wall and hidden from view by draping
  it over the inner wall level with the top
  two courses of brick. The coping is then
  mortared onto the edge of the liner

WILDLIFE POOLS

One of the undeniable attractions of water is to bring a greater variety of wildlife into the garden. This is increasingly important in urban gardens where many of the birds, mammals and insects, more often associated with the countryside, use a garden pool as a resting point in their busy search for food and water. Garden pools have become a major factor in slowing down the decline of several amphibians, insects and other creatures that can no longer find the right conditions in rural or agricultural environments. No matter how small the pool, leave an area of clear water for a week or two in the summer and, almost miraculously, a chain of life will start. Tiny, nearly microscopic, life appears at first, with the interest

growing over subsequent weeks as the pool becomes home to larger and larger invertebrates which arrive on the feet of birds or as eggs hidden away on new plants.

At the top of the food chain, there are several small mammals which are lured to a patch of water in the garden. Hedgehogs, badgers and foxes can often be seen at night, drinking from the pools in gardens, particularly in housing developments that are situated near the countryside. One of the most impressive sights in high summer are the huge dragonflies which dart and hover over the water, looking for shallow water in which to lay their eggs. It is a rich reward for the water gardener to see the freshly emerged ugly larva of a dragonfly turn into a winged beauty in a few hours.

BELOW: **Beneath the striking, pineapple-like tops of the water soldier (*Stratiotes aloides*), the clear water is teeming with life.**

RIGHT: Astilbes, heather (*Erica*) and honeywort (*Cerinthe*) make a pleasantly informal planting at the side of this cascade and provide shelter for visiting wildlife.

ABOVE: A raised decking path provides a good vantage point from which to view the wildlife attracted to this widened section of a shallow stream in a wild garden.

RIGHT: Common flag iris (*Iris pseudacorus*) and Bowles' golden sedge (*Carex elata* 'Aurea') provide cover as well as a home in which amphibians and birds can hide and feed.

A TRANQUIL WILDLIFE POOL

The lush informality of this pool makes it an attraction to wildlife. Although similar to an informal decorative pool, it has several design and construction points that are not apparent at first sight. The most important of these is the layer of soil on the pool bottom on top of the liner. This allows the ideal environment for several invertebrates to protect themselves in the mud. There are also several styles of edge to the pool, which allow easy access for amphibians. A small island is left undisturbed to allow rushes and sedges to cover the moist soil and create a safe haven for frogs and toads to bask in the sunshine. Although a compromise is evident in not having exclusively native plants, several of the marginals are indigenous, providing food for insects.

BELOW AND INSET: Marginals such as sweet galingale (*Cyperus longus*) jostle with giant rhubarb (*Gunnera manicata*) and the umbrella plant (*Darmera peltata*) to provide an excellent home for wildlife.

Island

2

3 4 5

5

6

1 7

15

9 8

12

10

11

13

14

Rock

Grass

Bark chipping
path around
edge of pool

PLANT LIST

1 *Iris sibirica*
2 *Gunnera manicata*
3 *Osmunda regalis*
4 *Phalaris arundinacea* var. *picta*
   'Feesey'
5 *Cyperus longus*
6 *Iris pseudacorus*
7 *Acorus gramineus*
   'Variegatus'
8 *Nymphaea tuberosa*
   (white waterlily)
9 *Nymphaea* 'René Gérard'
   (pink waterlily)
10 *Menyanthes trifoliata*
11 *Alchemilla mollis*
12 *Astilbe*
13 *Darmera peltata*
14 *Persicaria bistorta* 'Superba'
15 *Mimulus luteus*

USEFUL INFORMATION

MATERIALS

• Bark chippings: on one side of pool. If you create a bog garden to one side of the wildlife pool, then bark chippings are a very good surface for this boggy area. Bark chippings act as a mulch and help to retain moisture

• Occasional large rock to break up the grass edge of the pool

ISLAND CONSTRUCTION

• Islands can be added to the pool after construction, but this involves draining the pool first. For this reason, it is advisable to consider the inclusion of an island during the initial planning stages

• A flat-topped mound is created during the initial contouring of the excavation (the top of the mound should be finished at about 15cm/6in below the anticipated level of water in the pool)

• Turves stacked upside down on the edge of the island form a stable soil wall (heavy soil is added inside the turf wall)

• Plants in the wet soil soon develop a root system to bind the edges of the island

BOG GARDENS

A well-planted bog garden can look more natural in an informal setting than a tiny pool with a geometric shape and a ribbon of paving surrounding it. Bog gardens also provide the perfect method of introducing lushness to an otherwise arid landscape. The choice of plants that can be grown in boggy soils is often far more impressive in its diversity than the range of marginal plants available for small pools.

The bog garden is not simply an extension of the shallow water for marginal plants. It is an area of permanently moist soil rather than saturated soil, which allows some of the giants of the plant kingdom to make their impact in an informal garden. Including some plant giants in a patch of bog is a well-known method of making a garden look larger and more interesting. The plants associated with boggy areas are also enhanced enormously if they are reflected in an adjacent pool. However, a small bog garden may be considered a water feature in its own right, even if it is not associated with an adjacent area of clear water. It is certainly one of the least expensive types of water garden.

BELOW: **Candelabra primulas mix with Japanese iris (*Iris ensata*) to form a rich feeding station for insects in early summer.**

ABOVE: This access
bridge links a riot
of colour provided
by astilbes, iris and
primulas along the
sides of a stream.

LEFT: Bulrushes
(*Scirpus*) are perfect
bog plants, giving
height and form
to the plant mix,
while the giant
Himalayan cowslips
(*Primula florindae*)
and the variegated
figwort (*Scrophularia
auriculata* 'Variegata')
provide interest
in midsummer.

A SMALL BOG GARDEN

BELOW: **Bog gardens allow a wide range of lush leaf shapes and colours to maintain interest from early spring to autumn.**

INSET: **Access through this small bog garden is provided by log rounds, about 38cm (15in) in diameter and 30cm (12in) deep.**

A bog garden is a valuable water feature in a garden with light soil and little rainfall. Many of the plants are more traditionally used as marginals in shallow water, but, provided the soil is kept wet, most marginals will still flourish without a covering of water over the soil. Such a feature is ideal for the plantsperson who wishes to extend the range of plants that can be grown in an ordinary soil. Access is important to reach the plants as those conditions which encourage ample growth are also ideal for weeds, and deep-rooted weeds should not be allowed to gain a foothold. In this bog garden, access is provided by a stepping stone path of log slices through the centre of the feature. The fresh colours blend nicely and are ideal in a partly shaded site that is viewed regularly from a house window.

Grass

Stepping stones
using log slices

PLANT LIST

1 *Digitalis ferruginea*
2 *Cornus kousa* 'Snowboy'
3 *Carex elata* 'Aurea'
4 *Gunnera manicata*
5 *Iris sibirica*
6 *Scrophularia auriculata* 'Variegata'
7 *Primula florindae*
8 *Iris ensata*
9 *Ranunculus acris citrinus*
10 *Juncus ensifolius*
11 *Pontederia cordata*
12 *Primula japonica* 'Miller's Crimson'
13 *Epimedium davidii*
14 *Dierama pulcherrimum*
15 *Iris laevigata* 'Variegata'
16 *Viola sororia*
17 *Equisetum ramoissimum*
   var. *japonicum*
18 *Acorus gramineus* 'Variegatus'
19 *Peltandra undulata*

USEFUL INFORMATION

MATERIALS

• Thick bentomat liner: used here to
line the bog garden and made from
a sodium bentonite geocomposite.
Sodium bentonite is a naturally
swelling clay which expands to
12–15 times its dry volume when
it is fully hydrated. This makes it
a very useful sealant when the
swell pressure is contained in the
form of a clay liner. (Sodium bentonite
can also be used to create a watertight
seal between a pool and a bog garden.)

• "Rounds" of wood: measuring
approximately 38cm (15in) in
diameter and 30cm (12in) thick (the
rounds of wood should be spaced
about 23cm/9in apart and laid onto a
mixture of ballast and hardcore for
additional stability)

MAINTENANCE

• The bog garden will need to be kept
moist for the plants to thrive, so
periodically flood with a garden hose
during hot, dry weather

GRAVEL GARDENS

A gravel garden may seem, at first, to be incongruous in a garden associated with water. The Japanese were the first to use gravel to simulate water where water was either difficult to include or the aim was to stimulate the imagination. Large rocks were placed singly, and rake markings were created in the gravel to imitate the ripples of water. With the increasing popularity of gravel as a low-maintenance surface in dry areas in Western gardens, features like dried river beds can form either links between water features or schemes in their own right. With the additional benefits of planting, the watery impression can be quite dramatic.

A gravel garden may start as no more than a thin, meandering area, varying slightly in width, which is cut out of an existing lawn. As it is extended, larger plants can be introduced. If a weed blanket or landscape membrane were laid beneath the gravel, it would provide an extremely maintenance-free feature. Gravel gardens are often associated with arid settings, but, by choosing rounded rather than sharp gravel and including smooth boulders, an impression of moisture is much easier to achieve.

ABOVE RIGHT: **Gravel** and rock are a good combination in this sun-drenched terrace, which is flanked by lavender.

RIGHT: The illusion of water is created in an otherwise arid environment by rocks, gravel and a bridge.

OPPOSITE: These steps are made with gravel, timber and slate, and surrounded by a stunning mix of Himalayan poppies, Japanese maples (*Acer japonicum*), primulas and ferns.

A DRIED RIVER BED

Sometimes the illusion of water can make as satisfying a garden feature as the real thing, particularly where there is insufficient time to devote to maintaining water. Here, a dried river bed has been simulated, with the occasional pocket dug out for the moisture-loving plants. Mixed sizes of cobbles spread over a membrane both suppress weeds and act as a moisture-retaining mulch. The same mulch provides extra frost protection in the winter, allowing ornamental grasses a good start in the spring. The effect has been achieved by starting with a narrow bed at the highest point of the lawn and allowing this to widen as the bed travels down the gentle slope. A simple bridge makes a good crossing point halfway down, further adding to the illusion of water. The taller grasses are planted at the wider, lower section, giving the impression of a boggy zone.

INSET: **Grasses dominate this dried river bed, where the early rust-coloured flowers of *Calamagrostis* precede the *Miscanthus* which extend interest well into autumn with their flowerheads.**

BELOW: **Lower down, the bed suggests a boggy area where love grass (*Eragrostis*) and other moisture-loving grasses predominate.**

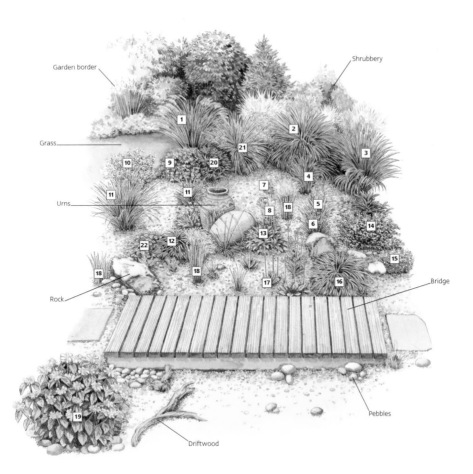

PLANT LIST

1 *Eragrostis curvula*
2 *Miscanthus sinensis* 'Gracillimus'
3 *Miscanthus sinensis* 'Sarabande'
4 *Miscanthus sinensis* 'Kleine Silberspinne'
5 *Echinacea purpurea* 'White Lustre'
6 *Sisyrinchium californicum*
7 *Campanula carpatica* 'Blaue Clips'
8 *Campanula fragilis*
9 *Oenothera kunthiana*
10 *Gypsophila paniculata*
11 *Poa labillardieri*
12 *Luzula acuminata*
13 *Luzula sylvatica*
14 *Prostanthera cuneata*
15 *Penstemon pinifolius* 'Wisley Flame'
16 *Luzula sylvatica* 'Aurea'
17 *Primula chungensis*
18 *Stipa tenuissima*
19 *Phlomis russeliana*
20 *Shibataea kumasasa*
21 *Libertia grandiflora*
22 *Viola canina*

USEFUL INFORMATION

MATERIALS

• Heavy duty polythene (polyethylene), such as old fertilizer or compost bags, for lining the planting holes for the vigorous, moisture-loving grasses

• Standard, ultra-violet-stabilized black polythene, 25 mucron (500 gauge) thick: used as a membrane to line the river bed (although it allows no movement of air and water except through planting holes, black polythene is an effective, low-cost means of controlling weeds as well as reducing water loss around new plants)

• Cobbles: these will protect the membrane from being damaged by ultra-violet light (without them it would degrade in approximately three years)

STREAMS AND CASCADES

BELOW: **The sound of a cascade brings life and vibrancy to the garden. It can be made noisier if the water plunges onto a shallow stream bed rather than into a deeper pool.**

The creation of a rocky informal stream epitomizes the most dramatic association of rock and water, and is the supreme challenge to the garden designer and landscaper. A stream brings noise and movement with infinite variations, allowing its impact to be gentle or dramatic. Streams are the ultimate water feature for the imaginative gardener; a small time spent by the side of a stream, listening to the sounds of the cascades and shallow rills, recharges the batteries and brings memories of favourite countryside walks. The home gardener can achieve these heights of creativity with relatively simple projects, particularly if natural streams and boulders have been used as the model.

As with many other products recently manufactured for the growing water-garden market, there are now several preformed stream units to make the construction process easier. Building a stream with cascades can seem daunting to the inexperienced, but the use of these units brings the feature within the scope of the most unskilled gardener. The style and appearance of these units are constantly being improved and now most types of rock are simulated in fibreglass. A more recent innovation is preformed stream units made from simulated cobbles and pebbles. Once the plants have become well established, it is often difficult to tell if a stream has been built using preformed units.

ABOVE: Elephants' ears (*Bergenia*) are good plants for dry soils at the streamside as they have lush-looking leaves even in drier conditions.

TOP: A smooth, ribbon-like cascade falling into a cobble-lined pool creates a more formal effect than a gushing waterfall.

LEFT: The pristine clarity of this stream is maintained during summer by the growth of oxygenating plants at the streamsides.

A CASCADING STREAM

The redevelopment of this garden, which involved the building of a new patio, provided a good opportunity to move an existing rigid pool and create a new stream. The main window of the house looks onto the patio and provides a perfect vantage point for viewing the gurgling stream on hot days. The newly planted surrounds of the stream will take a year or two to soften the rock edges and the rigid pool unit. The limestone rock used in the stream is more difficult to obtain and was originally bought for a rock garden some twenty years ago. The dismantling of old overgrown rock gardens often releases masses of expensive and weatherworn rock which has become increasingly rare and is particularly suitable for making a small stream with a flexible liner.

INSET: **A simple, flat, timber bridge, which is set into the path, accentuates the presence of the stream.**

RIGHT: **It is only a few weeks since the stream was constructed. The initial bareness of the base pool and the surrounding soil will soon be covered by the planting.**

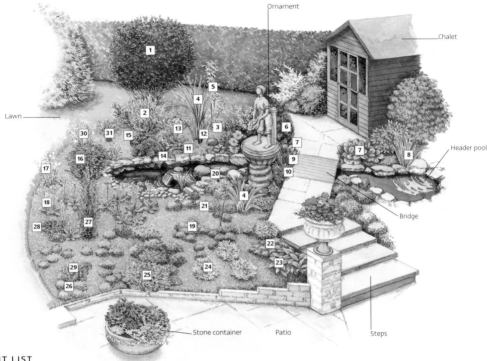

Ornament

Chalet

Lawn

Header pool

Bridge

Stone container   Patio   Steps

PLANT LIST

1 *Berberis thunbergii*
    'Atropurpurea'
2 *Artemisia absinthium*
    'Lambrook Silver'
3 *Brunnera macrophylla*
4 *Phormium tenax*
5 *Acer negundo*
    'Flamingo'
6 *Thuja orientalis*
7 *Bergenia cordifolia*
8 *Iris pseudacorus*
    'Variegata'
9 *Salvia officinalis*
    'East Freesland'
10 *Mimulus*
11 *Sedum*
12 *Iris sibirica*
13 *Astrantia major*
14 *Armeria*
15 *Cistus × skanbergii*
16 *Cistus × argenteus*
    'Peggy Sammons'

17 *Campanula alba*
    'Coronata'
18 *Primula beesiana*
19 *Erica carnea*
    'Springwood Pink'
20 *Dianthus deltoides*
21 *Erica carnea*
    'Springwood White'
22 *Erica carnea*
    'Winter Beauty'
23 *Viburnum davidii*
24 *Convolvulus cneorum*
25 *Helianthemum*
    'Rhodanthe Carneum'
26 *Erica carnea* 'Foxhollow'
27 *Taxus baccata*
    Fastigiata Aurea Group
28 *Fuchsia* 'Tom Thumb'
29 *Origanum laevigatum*
    'Herrenhausen'
30 *Cistus parviflorus*
31 *Olearia nummularifolia*

USEFUL INFORMATION

MATERIALS
- Rocks: 508kg (½ ton) of
  limestone pieces, each
  weighing 15–20kg (33–44lbs)
- Black corrugated plastic
  pipe, 2.5cm (1in) in
  diameter: used to circulate
  water to the top of the
  stream

TIMBER BRIDGE
To make a timber bridge,
measuring 1.2m (4ft) long:
- Lengths of decking cross
  planks, 60 x 15 x 2.5cm/
  24 x 6 x 1in

- Timber joists, 10 x 5cm/
  4 x 2in (length depends on
  width of stream): placed
  50cm (20in) apart onto
  which the cross planks are
  screwed at right angles
  (leaving a gap of 1cm/½in
  between planks)
- Concrete blocks on either
  side into which the joists
  are bedded

TYPE OF PUMP
- Submersible pump for base
  pool (flow rate of 3,645
  litres/963 gallons per hour)

A ROCK STREAM

An informal garden, where water's great attraction to birds is exploited in a stream and pool that almost enters the house, is viewed to the full through a large window, opening on to a small patio edging the pool. The garden is designed and maintained in a relaxed, informal style without too much attention placed upon manicured planting schemes. It is a place to be enjoyed from both inside and out.

The artificial rocks lining the stream are part of fibreglass stream units which have been beautifully disguised to the extent that they are extremely hard to identify among the real weathered rocks. There are shaded nooks and crannies almost hidden along the stream which provide permanent bathing pools for wildlife even when the pump is not operating.

This is a successful example of a design that reflects the owners' love of wildlife and colour.

INSET: **The rocks disguise the preformed stream units perfectly.**

LEFT: **The plant mix is bursting with vigour and seemingly nourished by the pool and stream, which are almost hidden by the lush vegetation.**

Shrubbery

Stream made from fibreglass units

Setts to edge of pool to allow "brimming pool" effect, with liner nipped between paving and setts; water is therefore maintained at maximum height

Paving

USEFUL INFORMATION

MATERIALS

- Rock: just over 508kg (½ ton) of 15–20kg (33–44lbs) limestone pieces to edge the pool and stream
- 3 rigid fibreglass stream units: lower unit (1m x 45cm x 15cm/3ft x 18in x 6in); double centre unit (1.2m x 45cm x 15cm/4ft x 18in x 6in)
- 1 rigid fibreglass header pool unit (1m/3ft in diameter, 30cm/12in deep)
- Base pool (3.6m x 1.8m x 60cm/ 12ft x 6ft x 2ft, with a volume of 3,406 litres/900 gallons)

TYPE OF PUMP

- Pump at base of waterfall (flow rate 3,645 litres/963 gallons per hour)

PLANT LIST

1 *Prunus*
2 *Anchusa azurea*
3 *Ajuga reptans*
4 *Geranium* 'Johnson's Blue'
5 *Sambucus serratifolia*
6 *Philadelphus coronarius*
7 *Hemerocallis*
8 *Oenanthe javanica* 'Flamingo'
9 *Erica × darleyensis* 'Silberschmelze'
10 *Cistus ladanifer*
11 *Lamium maculatum*
12 *Tulipa*
13 *Erigeron karvinskianus*
14 *Menyanthes trifoliata*
15 *Hosta fortunei* var. *aureomarginata*

16 *Caltha palustris* var. *palustris*
17 *Erigeron* 'Charity'
18 Pansy (*Viola × wittrockiana*)
19 *Elaeagnus angustifolia*
20 *Iris pseudacorus*
21 *Hyacinthoides non-scripta*
22 *Euphorbia polychroma*
23 *Vinca major*
24 *Prunus lusitanica*
25 *Nymphaea* 'Marliacea Chromatella'
26 *Calluna vulgaris* 'Antony Davis'
27 *Diascia* 'Ruby Field'
28 *Carex pendula*

SMALL WATER FEATURES

BELOW: **Constantly running water, cleverly contrived by a hidden reservoir and a pump, makes this** *tsukubai* **a captivating feature to watch.**

The trend towards smaller gardens has led to the increasing popularity of small-scale water features, which make little demand on space and which can fit into any style of garden. Many of these are free-standing, such as brimming urns, while others use moving water pumped from reservoirs hidden below ground. Most of these features require little or no maintenance, and are in tune with the lifestyle of the 21st century where there are so many other attractions to place demands on leisure time. The refreshment of water can be introduced at the flick of a switch.

Such features bring small spaces to life by providing a mixture of sound and movement, adding an element of surprise and a setting for interesting plant combinations. What these features have lost in the way of size, they have more than made up for in innovative design, unconventional materials and general appeal. They are often only discovered by visitors after a detailed exploration of the garden or by following the sound of trickling water. With little water exposed, there is much less danger to inquisitive children and, in fact, many water features can be mounted completely out of reach.

BELOW: The thin film of water constantly rippling from the centre of a millstone never ceases to fascinate.

ABOVE: This terracotta pot, which is being constantly replenished by a spout, is low in maintenance but high in impact.

LEFT: This white waterlily, *Nymphaea odorata* var. *minor*, not only provides flowers, but keeps the water clear with the shade cast by its leaves.

A COBBLE FOUNTAIN

A large garden with an expansive area devoted to lawn can be effectively broken by an informal gravel area, linking patio to grass. Such a design provides the perfect setting to include a cobble fountain among the plants and gravel, especially in the area most used for outdoor living. Gravel areas give great freedom to the planting, both in size of plant and their style. There is a nice mix of hardy and slightly tender plants so that if a severe winter damaged the less hardy specimens, the interest would still be maintained and any gaps made less conspicuous. The paving on the patio area is broken up slightly by replacing some of the paving slabs with the same cobbles used near the fountain. This provides a further link between the garden and the house.

INSET: **The water spout in this cobble fountain is made still more intriguing in the evening when it is illuminated by a spotlight.**

RIGHT: **Used as the mood dictates, the noise and movement of the small cobble fountain brings this corner of the garden to life.**

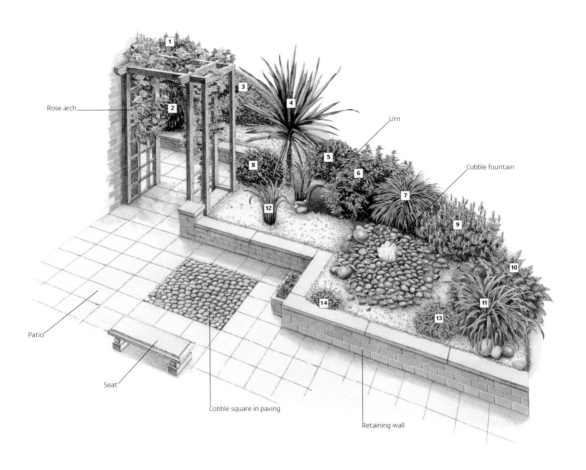

Rose arch

Urn

Cobble fountain

Patio

Seat

Cobble square in paving

Retaining wall

PLANT LIST

1 *Rosmarinus* 'Miss Jessopp's Upright'
2 *Thuja orientalis*
3 *Lonicera nitida* 'Baggesen's Gold'
4 *Cordyline australis*
5 *Rosmarinus* 'Benenden Blue'
6 *Cistus ladanifer*
7 *Miscanthus sinensis* 'Kleine Silberspinne'
8 *Cistus × skanbergii*
9 *Pinus mugo*
10 *Juniperus sabina* 'Tamariscifolia'
11 *Hemerocallis*
12 *Panicum virgatum*
13 *Carex siderosticha*
14 *Armeria maritima*

USEFUL INFORMATION

MATERIALS

- Rounded washed cobbles over the fountain grid
- Pea shingle or gravel: a 2.5cm (1in) deep layer to surround the fountain

LIGHTING

- 20 watt halogen light to illuminate the fountain spout (used below water or above ground) and capable of generating an intense beam of light at extremely low power consumption. The light is supplied with a weather-proof transformer with a 10m (30ft) cable and a 5m (16½ft) cable for the light. The light can be secured in the ground by stakes provided in the kit and there are optional colours for the lens. A yellow light gives the illusion of a flame

TYPE OF PUMP

- Submersible pump in the base of reservoir (flow rate of 1,000 litres/264 gallons per hour)

A BRIMMING URN

A simple stone seat by a brimming urn forms a lively point of interest in this seaside gravel garden. The gravel groundcover lies on a permeable membrane which prevents the weeds growing through, but, at the same time, allows water to reach the plants. This low-maintenance garden, which is able to survive the rigours of salty winds and low rainfall, is ideal for anyone with little time for gardening. Ornamental grasses dominate the planting, and extra interest in the gravel base is provided by undulating an otherwise flat garden. Odd pieces of driftwood collected from an adjacent beach add a final flourish.

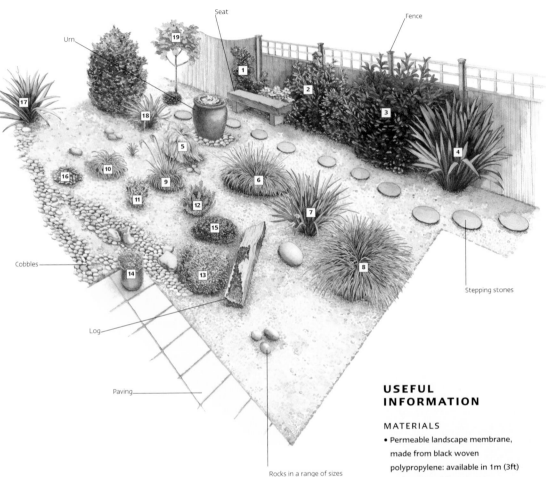

Seat

Urn

Fence

17

19

1

2

18

3

5

10

16

9

4

11

12

6

15

7

Cobbles

14

8

13

Stepping stones

Log

Paving

Rocks in a range of sizes

USEFUL INFORMATION

MATERIALS

- Permeable landscape membrane, made from black woven polypropylene: available in 1m (3ft) wide rolls; weight 100–110gms per sq. metre (3½oz per sq. yard)
- Urn (1m/3ft high and 45cm/18in at its widest diameter)
- Grades of gravel to cover membrane: 50mm (2in) and over, 40mm (1½in) and 30mm (1in)
- Log and rocks in a range of sizes

TYPE OF PUMP

- Submersible pump in a reservoir beneath the urn (flow rate of 1,560 litres/412 gallons per hour)

PLANT LIST

1 *Choisya ternata*
2 *Elaeagnus × ebbingei*
3 *Photinia × fraseri* 'Red Robin'
4 *Phormium tenax*
5 *Stipa tenuissima*
6 *Helictotrichon sempervirens*
7 *Iris foetidissima*
8 *Stipa arundinacea*
9 *Stipa gigantea*
10 *Carex oshimensis* 'Evergold'

11 *Teucrium fruticans*
12 *Picea glauca* var. *albertiana*
13 *Helianthemum* 'Wisley Primrose'
14 *Erigeron karvinskianus*
15 *Cryptomeria japonica* 'Spiralis'
16 *Skimmia japonica*
17 *Miscanthus sinensis* 'Variegatus'
18 *Imperata cylindrica* 'Rubra'
19 *Sorbus aria* 'Lutescens'

The choice of plants for the water and surrounding area is more than just an aesthetic consideration. The

PLANTING WATER AND ROCK GARDENS

health of a water feature depends on good planting, and oxygenating and shade plants should be a priority. Once these mainstays of the scheme are in place, there is scope for greater creativity, such as using plants to produce reflections in the water.

OPPOSITE: **The careful selection of aquatic plants makes this informal composition look natural rather than planned.**

PLANNING PLANTING SCHEMES

BELOW: **The choice and arrangement of the plants is of vital importance when you are designing a planting scheme for the waterside.**

The most commonly available aquatics are rampant native species, but they can be grown in small pools if they are containerized in aquatic planting baskets and divided regularly. Containers enable you to exploit the plants' lush growth, but at the same time prevent them from swamping the pool. Containers also allow a greater number of plants to be used in a small space.

Knowing the shape and colour of the leaves will be helpful in making your choice, because intensity of flower colour is not common in temperate aquatics. Visits to nurseries, flower shows and gardens will prove invaluable as you draw up a list of plants. However, a mixed planting scheme should not only blend your favourite species, but also keep together plants from the same type of habitat.

Maintaining interest all year round is a challenge in the water garden because most aquatics die down in late autumn and the old leaves turn straw-coloured. However, winter interest can be enhanced if the surrounding area is considered along with the surface of the water and its margins. In winter, the coloured stems and tree outlines come to the fore, making this one of the best times to enjoy reflections.

CHOOSING COLOURS

Although an informal pool allows greater freedom in the choice of plants than a formal one, it can soon become a tangled mix of uncoordinated plants and rank growth. The careful selection of shapes and more subdued colours are the chief attractions of an informal scheme, while stronger, more intense colours are more likely to be the focus in a formal pool. Subdued colours work well in temperate climates, where the pale tones and subtle textures harmonize with each other and are enhanced by the quality of the light.

Finding colours that harmonize can be difficult. It can be useful to refer to a colour wheel in order to help develop an appreciation of colour harmonies. Adjacent colours harmonize with each other because they share a pigment; opposite colours contrast with or intensify each other. You should also consider texture and tonal variations, which allow a much broader palette of colours to be used than appears in a simplified colour wheel. White waterlilies come in useful here, breaking up any potential clashes in colour harmony by reflecting light.

SPECIMEN PLANTING

An informal scheme lends itself to group plantings rather than to a collection of single specimens, but there is still a place for the occasional specimen plant, particularly in small schemes. Some excellent specimen plants include the arum lily (*Zantedeschia*), arrowhead (*Sagittaria*), horsetail (*Equisetum*), zebra rush (*Schoenoplectus lacustris* subsp. *tabernaemontani* 'Zebrinus'), and lizard's tail (*Saururus cernuus*). In tropical pools there are few plants to match the impact

FAR LEFT: **Where space permits, planting in groups is often more dramatic than specimen planting, especially with plants like this goatsbeard (***Aruncus***).**

LEFT: **Two classic and contrasting moisture-lovers jostle for space in this planting, the regal fern (***Osmunda***) forming a perfect background for the exotic Japanese iris (***Iris ensata***).**

of lotus (*Nelumbo*) as either a specimen or a group, with their combination of leaves like upturned umbrellas and brightly coloured flowers. Each of these plants combines an attractive shape with good flower colour.

PLANT DIVERSITY

The diversity of plants for water gardens is enormous. Leaf sizes range from the minuscule leaves of duckweed (*Lemna*) and watermeal (*Wolffia*) to the gigantic leaves of Amazonian waterlily (*Victoria amazonica*). The water garden includes some of the most beautiful flowers in the plant kingdom. Waterlilies (*Nymphaea*), for instance, display the most delicate, fragrant and exotic blooms, while lotus (*Nelumbo*) is surely one of the most exquisite combinations of leaf, flower and seed-heads.

The extent and speed with which floating plants can spread is equally dramatic. In warm, nutrient-rich tropical rivers plants such as water lettuce (*Pistia*) and water hyacinth (*Eichhornia*) can cover and choke vast areas of water in a single summer. Even in cooler temperate waters duckweed (*Lemna*) and fairy moss (*Azolla*) can cover the surface of a small pool in a matter of weeks. The nature of their habitat, where there is

constant water and food both in and around the margins of a pool, makes the careful choice of species particularly important. Many pools are spoiled when they become choked with vigorous species, which can be almost impossible to thin out if they are left unattended for two or three seasons.

GETTING THE BALANCE RIGHT

The construction of a new pool to encourage an increased range of wildlife to the garden or to create an architectural feature will require a diverse range of water plants if it is to be successful. Any expanse of fairly shallow water will quickly go green unless it is adequately stocked with plantlife or contains a sophisticated filtration system. The healthy, balanced pool depends on each layer of water depth being planted so that the water surface, the deep water and the shallow margins are inhabited with the particular type of plant that thrives in those conditions. The mixed planting will help in the establishment of a biological balance that contributes to clear water and provides a home for the myriad beneficial submerged organisms on which a natural food chain or eco-system depends.

PLANT TYPES AND ENVIRONMENTS

Water plants are categorized into the following groups: submerged, deep-water plants, floating plants and marginals. A successful planting scheme will include plants from each group, so that the pool and its immediate surroundings together form a complete environment. Achieving the correct balance among the plants is an important part of keeping the pool water clear and in preventing a build-up of algae.

SUBMERGED PLANTS

These plants are referred to as oxygenators. They are the workhorses or "weeds" of the pool, suppressing algae in their search for nutrients and providing a home for fish fry amid their strands of fine foliage.

The primary role of this group of aquatic plants is not aesthetic. It is to provide a living filtration system in the water through the leaves and roots. The leaves give off oxygen in the presence of sunlight, an important contribution to a pool that is heavily stocked with fish. In addition, the roots absorb nutrients from fish waste, thereby helping to prevent a build-up of toxic material and contributing to a balanced cycle of life within the pool. During the night, oxygenators deplete the water of oxygen and give off carbon dioxide, and this can result in some very low levels of oxygen during sultry nights in summer. This condition can be alleviated if there is a fountain in the pool and it is kept running through the night to help to replace lost oxygen.

RIGHT: *Eichhornia crassipes*, the water hyacinth, is a tender free-floating plant which will not survive winter outdoors in temperate climates. In very warm summers, it produces pale blue, hyacinth-like flowers, which grow to a height of 15–23cm (6–9in).

As well as supplying oxygen, these plants play a vital role in the water gardener's perennial battle with green water. Oxygenators seek nutrients from the water in the form of dissolved mineral salts, which are also the main diet of the tiny, single-celled algae that cause water to go green so quickly. If there are no oxygenators, the algae have no competition for their food. In a well-established pool the oxygenators leave few dissolved salts, and the algae are starved. It is for this reason that the water in a freshly constructed pool goes cloudy soon after the pool is filled. Even if oxygenators are introduced at once, mineral salts are present in high concentrations in tap-water and the young plants will have made inadequate growth to use them up. This can be the most frustrating time for new pool owners, and many people are tempted to change the water in an effort to return to clear water. This desire must be resisted at all costs, because the problem will certainly recur shortly after replacing the water if tapwater is used. The answer is to be patient, and quite unexpectedly, the pool will become clear as quickly as it clouded weeks before. The algae will have been starved out and are unlikely to reappear unless large volumes of tapwater are introduced.

Sometimes the oxygenators can grow beyond the surface of the water and creep out into the margins. A plant called diamond milfoil (*Myriophyllum aquaticum*) is particularly prone to this aerial growth, and when the leaves are as attractive as those of milfoil, there is no harm in letting it sprawl. It is, however, essential to cut it back in autumn because the decaying, frost-damaged leaves will blacken and rot in the water, which has the effect of deoxygenating the water. This autumn cutting back of vigorous growth applies to all the other oxygenators.

Good aquatic centres will usually have about six species of oxygenator from which you can choose, and they are mainly native plants. Buy several species so that if any one type fails, it is likely that another will flourish. They are normally sold as bunches of unrooted cuttings with a weight, used as the clasp to keep the cuttings together and prevent them from floating if they become dislodged from the bottom. More oxygenators are now being sold in small cubes of rockwool so that they can be just thrown into the pool and will develop in the small amount of soil that inevitably accumulates on the bottom.

If you are planting in containers, keep the same species together so that vigorous types do not smother more delicate ones. If you are using a planting crate, bear in mind that a medium-sized crate will hold five bunches, one in the centre and one in each corner. For a new pool, aim for five bunches to every square metre (10 square feet) of pool surface.

Many oxygenators have exquisite foliage, which, when it is submerged, does not require fibrous tissue to maintain its shape. When suspended in water, the leaves are often thin and translucent. Some genera, such as *Cabomba*, are used in aquaria because of the delightful arrangement of their whorled leaves. In outdoor pools the fine leaves of oxygenators make superb retreats for fish fry to escape the cannibalism of larger fish. The leaves also make hidden depositories for fish eggs.

ABOVE: **The young leaves of autumn starwort (***Callitriche hermaphroditica***), an oxygenating plant, are a delicacy for goldfish.**

FLOATING PLANTS

Although there are several aquatic plants with floating leaves, this group contains free-floating plants that are not anchored to the bottom. Wherever you see this type of plant, the water will invariably be crystal clear. The floating leaves will have so reduced the amount of daylight entering the water that insufficient of the sun's energy is available for the algae to survive. The suspended, fine, hair-like roots of floating plants also use up considerable quantities of dissolved nutrients at the surface of the water where algae would otherwise flourish. This makes them useful in establishing a newly constructed pool. Some floating plants have extensive fine roots which make homes for fish fry and tiny, almost microscopic, life. Newly introduced fish also like the protective surface cover, especially in a new pool where the submerged plants have not yet developed.

The main problem is the ability of floaters to colonize large surfaces of water. In some tropical and subtropical countries it is illegal to introduce these plants to waterways, which become completely impassable. In a large natural pool, therefore, floaters should be introduced with great care. In smaller pools, where the plants can be easily netted off, the advantages outweigh any problems. In temperate climates most species sink to the bottom in winter, reappearing in the warmer spring days by floating to the surface.

In addition to contributing to clear water, many floating plants are extremely attractive in their own right, especially when they are viewed at close quarters on the surface of a raised pool.

One of the most common examples of a floating plant in temperate climates is duckweed (*Lemna*). There are different types of duckweed. It exhibits an extraordinary ability for rapid reproduction by offsets, which is the most common method for this group of plants, and can be something of a pest in a large ornamental pool. However, the smaller, ivy-leaved species, *L. trisulca*, is less invasive. For warmer pools the tender water hyacinth (*Eichhornia*) has the bonus of a flower that can be produced if the weather is very hot and sunny for a prolonged period. Because there is such a small choice of hardy floaters, you may have to use the more tender species that have only a limited time outdoors in temperate pools. As most of these become available only when the water is really warm in early summer, they are on sale for a limited time.

There are two other tender floaters: fairy moss (*Azolla*) and water lettuce (*Pistia*). The tender species will probably die out in winter and are unlikely to cover too much of the pool's surface. Fairy moss will sink to the bottom as spores, reappearing in spring if conditions are right. Keep water hyacinth and water lettuce indoors in a light, airy, frost-free place. The plants survive best when left on a muddy seed tray rather than in cold water.

Planting floaters is simple. Empty out the bag of plants on to the surface of the water. The water hyacinth and water lettuce may exhibit an initial lack of buoyancy if they have been in a bag for some time, but they will soon right themselves. In an exposed pool they tend to be blown all over the surface, but can be kept together in a floating wooden frame, anchored to the bottom.

DEEP-WATER PLANTS

The plants in this group grow in deep water, which is usually defined as water 30–60cm (12–24in) deep in ornamental pools. Although waterlilies (*Nymphaea*) are the best known example of this group, they are often given a section of their own in catalogues, leaving a small selection of other plants that have surface leaves but roots that are anchored in the deeper water.

Deep-water plants are grown not only for their flowers but also for the valuable shade that is cast by their leaves in summer, which makes a contribution to clear water at a time it is most needed. The leaves in this group are floating and flat, providing resting platforms for a variety of creatures and, on the undersides, a depository for eggs. The leaves prefer still water and, unlike the totally submerged plants, are less tolerant of currents. They can survive the worst temperate winters because the thick rhizomes are below the ice layer.

Deep-water plants are particularly beneficial because they both decorate the pool and provide shade. Fish and other aquatic creatures enjoy this shade, and it can provide useful cover when herons are regular visitors. When you are creating a planting plan for the pool's surface, aim to cover between one-third to one-half of the water with leaves. Intersperse clumps of plants with equal areas of clear water to provide the best effect, because a pool completely dominated by surface leaves loses much of its impact. A good plant for deeper water is Cape pondweed or water hawthorn (*Aponogeton distachyos*). In addition to its dark green, strap-like leaves, this intriguing plant produces scented white flowers earlier than the waterlilies,

with a second flush in autumn as the water cools down. For this reason, *Aponogeton* is recommended for pools where there is inadequate sunshine for waterlilies to flower successfully.

New deep-water plants should be purchased in late spring, just as growth has started. Avoid disturbing plants in winter in case a cut or damaged root begins to rot in the cold water rather than healing quickly as it is more likely to do when in active growth. Deep-water plants are often sold as bare-rooted specimens, having been freshly divided from the parent plant. Buying containerized plants saves root disturbance, but established plants in containers are heavy and the extra expense is seldom justified as bare-rooted plants soon catch up in growth if they are planted at the right time. Deep-water plants require good root systems so that the nutrient reserves support the leaves as they try to reach the surface, and the largest size of planting crate should be used. Try to provide at least 30 litres (about 8 gallons) of compost (soil mix) in a crate about 40cm (16in) in diameter and 20cm (8in) deep. A larger container is even better.

WATERLILIES

Although classified as deep-water plants, waterlilies are generally given a section of their own. The beauty of the waterlily has exercised the skills of the writer and painter alike, with its perfect blooms, subtle perfume and range of colours, which change slightly each day in the flower's brief life on the surface. It is not only the exquisite blooms that make the waterlily the most popular aquatic plant, but also the spread of the leaves, which provide vital shade in high summer.

Waterlilies are divided into hardies and tropicals, with the tropicals further divided into day- and night-blooming plants. Hardy forms can remain outdoors in temperate winters quite satisfactorily, even if the surface of the water is frozen for significant periods. The tropicals, which tend to hold their flowers above the surface of the water, are often treated as annuals, particularly in climatic zones that are only marginally tropical.

Waterlily breeding is going through something of a revival, particularly in North America, where tropicals can be grown in the southern states. All waterlilies enjoy full sun and still, warm water, which should be free from the turbulence of a fountain or strong winds. A little time spent dead-heading and removing old and yellowing leaves will be amply rewarded by more flowers, and the sight of overgrown leaves thrusting above the surface and very few flowers is a sign of neglect.

Like the marginal plants, waterlilies can be planted in three ways, but by far the most common method is to use containers. Different waterlilies vary considerably in vigour and the depth of water in which they will thrive.

MARGINALS

The fringe of the water garden is home to a group of plants that play a vital part in the aesthetic impact of the pool. The shallow water and the nearby water-logged soil are inhabited by marginals, which thrive in various conditions, from having hardly any water at one extreme to having a depth of water 15–23cm (6–9in) above their root systems. The plants in this latter group tolerate different amounts of water over their root systems, and it is important not to drown the very shallow water plants. Short or seasonal variations in water level can be tolerated, and deciduous shallow-water marginals will tolerate more water in winter over their crowns than in summer. Slightly deeper water in winter also helps to protect plants such as arum lilies (*Zantedeschia*) from severe frost and winds. Vigorous species of marginal will be prevented from invading the centre of the pool if the water is too deep for them to survive, hence the importance of having marginal shelves only 23cm (9in) deep in a new pool. Natural

LEFT: **The Amazon waterlily (***Victoria amazonica***) makes a striking addition to a tropical pool. It should be grown at a minimum temperature of 25°C (77°F).**

pools with shallow, saucer-shaped sides will gradually become swamped by vigorous marginals, such as reedmace (*Typha*) and reeds (*Phragmites*), which form floating rafts of thick root systems that will eventually encroach on the centre of the pool.

The range of marginal plants has for many years been limited to a core list of indigenous species, but as interest in water gardening has expanded, so the range of available marginals has become more extensive. There is now a greater international exchange of

FAR LEFT: **Irises must rank as one of the waterside favourites, for both wet and moist soil.**

LEFT: **The familiar florists' arum lily (***Zantedeschia***) is hardier when it is just submerged to protect the crown. Graceful Z. *aethiopica* 'Crowborough' is ideal for situations such as this.**

ABOVE: **As the soil becomes less saturated away from the margins of the pool, there are several moisture-loving iris, such as the Siberian iris (*Iris sibirica*), which are suitable for such conditions and best planted in drifts.**

RIGHT: **The flowers of candelabra primulas look stunning against a dark background.**

looked after more easily as competition for space becomes more intense. The fast rate of growth of the indigenous marginals is not always considered when space is allocated for different plants. Tempting though it is to have an established pool quickly, if too many rampant growers are close together, the lush growth will obscure the light and compete for space with the smaller plants, and the ultimate height that some of these plants achieve may be out of scale when there is only a small surface area visible. If the taller plants are planted into small, inadequate containers, their lank, sappy growth will make them susceptible to being blown over, and you will probably have to re-pot them in a matter of weeks. Many of the species that grow to 1–1.2m (3–4ft) are more appropriate to larger wildlife pools, where they can be planted directly into the soil. Make sure that around smaller ornamental pools there are sufficient carpeting species, such as speedwell or brooklime (*Veronica*), to help soften edges and keep the growth in scale with the area of the pool.

MOISTURE-LOVING PLANTS

The plants in this group are not strictly aquatic plants, but they play a crucial role in the successful transition from the water to the drier regions of the garden. Moisture-lovers are mainly used in informal water gardens in the rich soil that has ample reserves of water without being waterlogged. Although many of them will survive in drier soils, their performance in both size and flowering never reaches the same potential if they do not have adequate and constant moisture.

Several woody plants are included in this group, such as dogwood (*Cornus*), alder (*Alnus*) and willow (*Salix*). These species should be planted in the same way as ordinary terrestrial plants: dig out a planting hole, add moisture-retentive organic matter and firm in the roots. Unlike aquatics, which are planted in the growing season, moisture-loving plants are best planted in autumn or spring.

OTHER POOLSIDE PLANTS

The emphasis in any water-garden planting is naturally given to the main groups of plants that can thrive in aquatic conditions. The planting in the immediate surrounds where the soil can be quite dry is equally important if the full potential of the design is to be realized. Trees and shrubs form the framework to water gardens, providing height, which in turn creates a sense of scale. There is such a wide diversity in the

species, and breeding programmes of specialist growers have introduced new cultivars, notably of *Iris*, monkey flower (*Mimulus*) and *Lobelia*. Towards the end of summer, displays of marginals not only look depleted, they often look starved, and it is best to avoid making new purchases at this time of year. Buy in spring or early summer when the plants have fresh new growth thrusting from the compost (soil mix), and they will quickly become established in the pool as the days get longer and the water warms up.

For your initial planting, choose the well-tried native species because they will grow well and require little pampering. Save some of the prime positions for special favourites or for less vigorous plants that can be

characteristics of trees and shrubs, that there can be few water gardens that would not benefit from their inclusion in one form or another.

One of the main advantages of woody plants in an aquatic surround is the winter interest. As aquatics and moisture-loving herbaceous plants die down in winter, the woody stems persist on shrubs, and, when these are coloured or form a tracery of branches, they come into their own among dead, brown vegetation. In addition to winter interest, the use of woody plants can exploit reflection. The light bark colours of certain birch species are very useful in this respect and large shrubs or small trees with catkins are also most effective.

Although deciduous trees are associated with leaves blowing into the water in autumn, their dappled shade can be a valuable compensation for the margins of some pools. There are several moisture-loving plants that scorch badly in full sun, and the dappled light below trees is ideal for these plants. Avoid planting the very thirsty species of trees and shrubs, like many willows and poplars, close to a pool. If a liner weeps moisture from the slightest imperfection in the manufacture, the roots of adjacent trees will find this water and inevitably make the seepage worse in time.

Conifers are valuable in providing single specimens for reflection or making hedges to enhance a formal scheme and providing shelter from wind. Avoid siting a pool too near overhanging branches as, despite retaining their leaves in the winter, they constantly shed bud scales and needles, making the water surface very dusty. There are several slow-growing, dwarf conifers that can be grown amongst rocks at the side of a watercourse. As many of them are quite tolerant of dry conditions, they make a good choice for raised mounds of soil for rock gardens where there is limited moisture and it is much harder for roots to reach the water table.

GRASSES AND FERNS

There is a particular affinity between the waterside and ornamental grasses and ferns. The very fine flowers of grasses can be lost in a mixed border where the variety of colours and leaf shapes make the detail of the flowers difficult to see. Provide a backdrop of a water surface and their effect is enhanced. Some of the grasses that actually like quite dry conditions can also be used in an informal setting to suggest a boggy area without the soil being at all moist. Where there is ample moisture, there are numerous species of ornamental rushes and sedges that will occur naturally by water.

LEFT: **Bowles' golden sedge (*Carex elata 'Aurea'*) is a striking marginal, which is grown for its bright golden yellow leaves.**

ALPINES

There are few informal schemes where rock and water are combined that would not look very stark and bare without alpines. The soil edges immediately outside lined pools are the classic situation for scrambling types of alpine. These plants are adapted to use the available moisture present in the soil in late winter and spring to flower and seed quickly in native habitats which dry out as the summer progresses. The scrambling types will be of greatest use to the water gardener as they soften and hide stream and pond edges and bring a riot of colour to a rock formation in spring.

BELOW: **The daisy-like fleabane (*Erigeron karvinskianus*) is a superb plant, which will seed itself among the crevices and dry crannies in rocks.**

PLANTING AQUATICS

Unlike terrestrial plants, water plants have no need to develop an extensive root system to seek out moisture. As the planting medium is permanently waterlogged, the need for drainage or moisture-retaining materials in the compost (soil mix) is superfluous. This means that quite large plants can be grown in relatively small containers specially adapted for aquatic growth. As this growth is rapid for a short season, the vigorous species will need dividing and replanting every year with fresh compost.

AQUATIC PLANTING CRATES

Planting baskets for aquatics are available in a variety of shapes and sizes, and they differ from ordinary plant containers in having lattice sides, which make it possible for the gases and chemicals that are produced in the compost (soil mix) to pass easily into pool water and so prevent the soil inside the container from stagnating. In addition to the round crates, there are also square and curved ones, which are ideal for standing on a curved marginal shelf. The wider the base of the planting basket, the more stable it will be, and this is important if a tall plant is likely to be

OPPOSITE: **A planting basket placed on the marginal shelf allows the plant to be immersed at just the right depth.**

buffeted by wind. These planting baskets are made of plastic, and although they are mostly black, you can sometimes buy green ones.

To prevent the compost (soil mix) in the basket from leaching out into the water, the baskets are lined with a permeable lining, such as hessian (burlap) or polypropylene mesh. Liners are sold at aquatic centres, ready cut into squares of different sizes. More expensive containers are available that have smaller louvred mesh sides, and these do not need a lining.

The containers range from 40cm (16in) in diameter, which are suitable for medium to large waterlilies, to 4cm (1½in) in diameter, which are used for cuttings or aquarium plants. The vigorous plants soon become potbound and suffer through having insufficient nutrients, and the regular division and repotting of these plants into fresh compost (soil mix) is essential.

PLANTING MEDIUM

Soil suitable for aquatic plant containers can be taken from the garden, provided the soil is not too rich in nutrients and is free from pesticide and herbicide residues. The soil should preferably be on the heavy

TYPES OF AQUATIC PLANTING BASKET

There are aquatic planting baskets for every type of aquatic, from vigorous waterlilies to small oxygenators. Some baskets are contoured to fit on the shelves of curving preformed units.

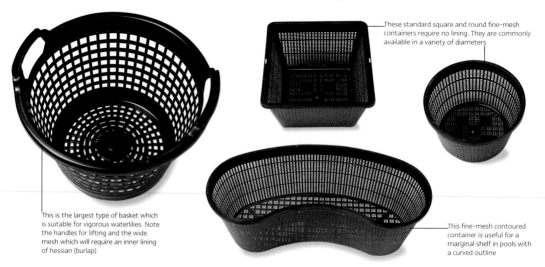

These standard square and round fine-mesh containers require no lining. They are commonly available in a variety of diameters

This is the largest type of basket which is suitable for vigorous waterlilies. Note the handles for lifting and the wide mesh which will require an inner lining of hessian (burlap)

This fine-mesh contoured container is useful for a marginal shelf in pools with a curved outline

side and neither extremely acid nor extremely alkaline. Avoid peaty soils, which decompose very rapidly, or sandy soils which have little or no nutrient value. If your soil is a heavy loam, it will probably be suitable. If you are using garden soil, sieve it through a coarse sieve to remove stones and any loose organic matter. An ideal home-made aquatic compost (soil mix) can be made from old turves that have been stacked for a few months and are rotting down into a condition described as a fibrous loam.

Proprietary multi-purpose or soil-based composts (soil mixes) should be avoided, because these contain too many nutrients and materials that are not necessary for submerged conditions.

If you are uncertain whether your garden soil is suitable, you can buy bags of aquatic compost (soil mix). The content of these proprietary aquatic composts can vary enormously, and they are expensive if you have a large pool to plant.

PLANTING TIME

Aquatics should be planted while in growth and not touched during their dormant period. The warmer the water, the more quickly the new plant will become established, and the ideal time is late spring when there is plenty of sunshine, long hours of sunlight and

OTHER PLANTING EQUIPMENT

Other pieces of equipment, such as long-sleeved gloves and planting mats and liners for aquatic planting baskets, will prove very useful when planting up a water garden.

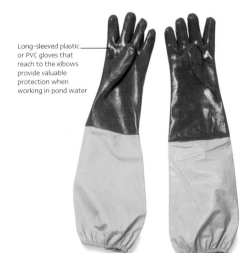

Long-sleeved plastic or PVC gloves that reach to the elbows provide valuable protection when working in pond water

Border planting mats made from natural jute or coconut material can be draped over the muddy margins of a pool to provide extra grip for pond plants and to help prevent erosion. They will degrade in the water over two years

Hessian (burlap) liners can be cut into squares for baskets of different diameters. They prevent the compost (soil mix) from escaping through the sides of the container. Very steep pond borders can also be covered in this finer-weave material to make planting pockets which will rot in time when the plant roots have stabilized the banks

warmer water. If the planting is left until autumn, the water will still be warm, but will be gradually cooling down and the plant may not have time to become established before winter. If the temperature falls sharply and the plants are slightly tender, as are some waterlilies, they will not have had sufficient time to build up reserves in their root systems. If containerized plants are bought, the planting time is less important.

DIRECT PLANTING

In a natural or wildlife pool with a minimum covering of 15cm (6in) of soil over the liner, aquatics can be planted directly into this soil. In such conditions plants will spread rapidly, and direct planting is ideal only in very large pools where there is a deep area of water into which the plants cannot spread and which prevents the entire pool from becoming overgrown. A

RIGHT: **A good mixture of marginals and alpines is essential for a rocky watercourse in which extremes of dry and moist soils are found.**

small pool can be planted by this method, but the range of suitable plants is limited and regular cutting back will be essential.

PERMANENT PLANTING BEDS

These beds are better suited to large pools, where the number of aquatic containers might be excessive. The beds can be free-standing in the deep water near the centre for plants like waterlilies, or built with a retaining wall to enclose the soil between the side of the pool and the wall. The retaining walls can be built with a variety of natural and man-made materials such as rocks, walling stones, bricks and concrete blocks. If the walls are mortared for extra strength to resist the pressure of roots, it is important that small holes are left in the sides for gases and salts in solution to escape into the water. The walls can be built onto flexible liners, and if this is done the liner should be protected by a layer of polythene (polyethylene) or by a spare piece of liner. The top of the walls should finish a few centimetres under the water level so that they are not seen.

DEPTH OF PLANTING

Most marginal plants will tolerate a certain depth of water above their crown or growing point when they are placed on a marginal shelf in a container. However, the question of depth is more important when you are planting waterlilies, which vary considerably in their tolerance. If you buy from a reliable aquatic supplier, the information will be printed on the plant label, and if you are in any doubt, ask the supplier. The suggested depth will refer to the depth of water above the growing point or crown; it does not refer to the base of the container. Err on the side of shallow planting rather than immersing the plant too deeply, especially with a young, bare-rooted waterlily that has just been containerized.

The danger of planting too deeply in the early stages can be avoided by propping up the container on some bricks or blocks on the floor of the pool so that the growing point is covered by no more than 10–15cm (4–6in) of water. As the plant begins to grow, the bricks can be removed one by one from the supporting pier beneath until, by the time the plant is growing strongly, the container is resting on the bottom of the pool.

If young plants are planted into permanent beds, the water level should be reduced initially, then topped up gradually as the plants get stronger.

PERMANENT PLANTING BED

Marginal planting beds, which are permanent, can be made with bricks or walling stones. This type of planting bed is suitable for formal ponds.

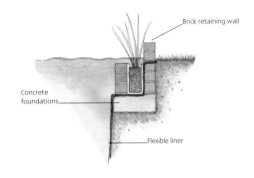

Brick retaining wall

Concrete foundations

Flexible liner

TEMPORARY PLANTING

A planting basket placed on a marginal shelf can be used to help amphibians gain access to and from the pool if a roofing tile or small slab is placed on the compost (soil mix).

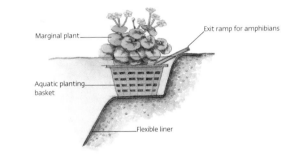

Marginal plant

Exit ramp for amphibians

Aquatic planting basket

Flexible liner

PLANTING DEPTHS

Young waterlilies in planting baskets should be supported on a brick pier at first before being placed on the bottom of the pool when they are growing vigorously.

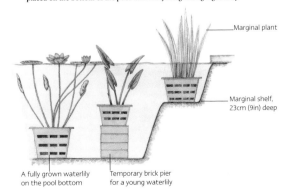

Marginal plant

Marginal shelf, 23cm (9in) deep

A fully grown waterlily on the pool bottom

Temporary brick pier for a young waterlily

PLANTING TECHNIQUES

Aquatic plants can be planted in a number of ways: in aquatic crates, in permanent beds or directly in the soil. The method depends on whether you are planting a submerged or deep-water aquatic, a marginal or a moisture-lover. If you are planting in a basket, the golden rule is always to firm in the compost (soil mix) well. If this is not done, there will be a great reduction in volume when the compost is submerged and large amounts of air are expelled.

OXYGENATORS

If oxygenators are purchased as bunches of unrooted cuttings and are to be planted in a newly installed pool, they will stand a better chance of survival and will begin to develop more readily if they are planted in a container. A medium-sized container, about 20cm (8in) square, will be adequate. It should be lined with a square of permeable material, such as hessian (burlap) or polypropylene, and filled to the brim with soil or aquatic compost (soil mix). Firm down the compost, make some holes with a dibber (dibble), then push the bunches into position. They are usually best arranged with one in the centre and one in each corner, and the bottom of the stems should be just buried. Firm in the stems and top-dress the compost with a layer of washed pea gravel about 2.5cm (1in) thick.

The gravel not only prevents soil particles from floating about when the container is immersed but also stops inquisitive fish from disturbing the surface of the soil. Place the containers on the bottom of the pool as quickly as possible after planting, because the plants curl up very quickly when they are out of water.

If the pool is well established, weigh down the bunches with a small weight which holds the ends of the stems together, and throw them into the centre of the pool, where they will settle into the thin layer of mud on the bottom. Individual plants bought in plugs of rockwool can be simply thrown into the pool.

PLANTING AN OXYGENATOR

The unrooted cuttings of oxygenating plants will flourish best in a new pond if they are first planted in an aquatic container before being placed at the bottom of the pond.

1 Fill a small planting crate with aquatic planting compost (soil mix) to the brim of the container.

2 Using a wooden dibber (dibble), make a hole in the centre of the compost (soil mix) deep enough for the bunch of oxygenating plants to be inserted so that the clasp holding the bunch together is buried in the compost.

3 Firm the compost (soil mix) around the bunch thoroughly so that there is no danger of it floating out when the container is submerged.

4 Place a layer of small chippings or washed pea shingle or gravel over the top of the compost (soil mix). This prevents the particles of soil escaping into the water and gives some protection from inquisitive fish. Immerse in the pond as soon as possible because the soft leaves of submerged plants will desiccate very rapidly when out of water.

MARGINALS

These plants can be planted in three main ways: in a special planting basket, in a permanent bed or directly in the soil at the bottom of the pond. Most are planted into planting crates of various sizes, which makes it possible to move them around on the marginal shelves. The size of the container will relate to the vigour of the plant, because this will determine its ultimate spread and height.

When you are choosing the container, take into account how much restraint is required and the depth of water in which the container is to be positioned. Many marginals require only shallow water over their crowns, and this factor will affect the depth of the container when it is standing on a typical marginal shelf, 23cm (9in) deep. Ensure that the plant is securely held in the soil, which must be covered with a good layer of gravel if it is to be submerged. Do not bury the roots too deeply and ensure that they are spread out adequately in the container.

Marginals can also be planted into permanent beds, which are constructed when the pool is built. Permanent planting beds can be built behind the rocks when constructing a pond, or more substantial planting beds can be made by building retaining walls with brick or walling stones. These are made when the pool is originally constructed and should be built so that the tops of the retaining walls are just below the waterline. Planting into this type of permanent bed allows some intermingling of species and looks more natural. Greater care is required in the plant choice and positioning so that the vigorous species do not overrun their neighbours.

Some marginals can be planted in the soil that covers the whole submerged area of a wildlife pool. There are no restrictions on the root systems of such plants, which will spread very rapidly. This may be acceptable in a wildlife pool but is not recommended in a small ornamental pool.

PLANTING A MARGINAL

Marginals can be planted in a planting basket and then submerged in the pond.

1 Half-fill a medium-size planting crate with aquatic planting compost (soil mix).

2 Check that there is ample depth in the container to bury the plant to the same depth as its previous planting, taking care not to bury too deeply.

3 Place the plant near the centre of the container and add the compost (soil mix) so that the loose compost reaches the rim.

4 Firm the compost (soil mix) thoroughly around the roots and base of the leaves.

5 Spread a layer of washed pea shingle or gravel over the compost (soil mix) to prevent the soil particles from floating.

6 Place the freshly potted plant on to the marginal shelf of the pond.

WATERLILIES AND OTHER DEEP-WATER AQUATICS

Some waterlilies have thick, flattish, creeping roots; others have pineapple-shaped roots. When planting, the fleshy rhizomes of the creeping root type should be laid horizontally under about 2.5cm (1in) of soil, while the more upright, pineapple-shaped root is planted vertically or at a slight angle, with the crown or growing point almost exposed at the surface. Whatever the type of root, ensure the crown is planted shallowly.

Before planting, trim off the fibrous roots and examine the root carefully for any signs of damaged or diseased tissue. Cut out any suspicious material and dust the exposed tissue with fungicide. The leaves are often damaged in transport, and it is far better to remove these leaves before planting than to allow them to rot off. Even if all the foliage is dead or damaged, the plant can still survive at planting time. During planting, keep the foliage cool and damp, and never leave plants exposed to sun or drying wind.

When you are planting a waterlily in a container, choose a large size of crate, and firm the soil thoroughly around the rootstock because, once all the air is expelled by firming and the soil is saturated, the volume will shrink considerably. If the soil has been inadequately firmed, containers will only be half full a short time after immersing. It is, therefore, a good idea to water thoroughly before planting and to add any extra soil that may be needed. Finally, when the soil has been firmed, add a layer of pea gravel about 2.5cm (1in) deep. Plant shallowly, using bricks under the container, which can be gradually removed when growth starts. Containerized planting for deep-water plants largely follows the method described above for waterlilies.

The technique for planting tropical waterlilies is similar to that for hardy plants, although it varies in a few important ways. The tropicals are generally more vigorous and faster growing than the hardy plants, and they should be given large containers. In most temperate climates their cultivation

PLANTING A WATERLILY

Increasingly, waterlilies are being sold in aquatic baskets ready for planting; these will be adequate until the plant needs dividing.

1 Do not plant the young containerized plant too deeply until it is established. Build a temporary brick pier so that the top of the container will be approximately 15cm (6in) below the surface of the water.

2 Remove any old or damaged leaves which will soon rot in the water. Gently place the container on top of the support.

3 As the plant grows and the leaf stems elongate, remove one layer of bricks at a time until the plant is strong enough to be placed on the pool bottom.

is restricted to pools in conservatories where water temperatures of 24–29°C (75–85°F) can be guaranteed. In temperatures below 21°C (70°F) the young tropicals frequently go dormant. In temperate climates they should be planted later than the hardy waterlilies so that the warmer water will encourage rapid development.

The hardy plants are sold as rootstocks of the parent plant, but tropicals are sold as complete young plants. These are planted into containers as described for

the hardies, but a sachet of slow-release fertilizer should be added to the planting medium. They are planted shallowly and, unlike the hardies, do not need to be gradually introduced to deeper water. They flourish in surface water that warms up quickly in the sun. For both hardy and tropical waterlilies, anticipate the problem of reaching the deeper area of the pool with a container full of compost (soil mix) which is often heavy. For larger pools, you will need to wear waders to reach the deeper area.

MOISTURE-LOVERS

These plants are usually planted in soil that is not saturated at the edges of the pool. For this reason, they are treated in the same way as other herbaceous plants. Moisture-loving plants are frequently planted in soil conditions which will be compacted if you are working in one area for any length of time and it is useful to work from temporary planks or permanent stepping stones, such as partially buried railway sleepers (ties), for access to the planting bed.

NON-AQUATIC PLANTS

Disguising the edges of rigid stream units and informal preformed pools is often difficult as the soil can be quite dry in these areas. The technique for planting these areas involves procedures which are almost completely opposite to those required for aquatics. Whereas aquatic plants will have no need to develop an extensive root system in search of water, the terrestrial plants will need help in their initial stages to survive and grow in a dry environment, particularly when planted on any form of raised soil bed like a rock garden. At the same time as needing water to grow, these plants also need good drainage in order for oxygen to be available for the roots, an element which aquatics are specially adapted to take in through leaves or roots when present in the pool water.

The steps for planting shown here will assume that the plants are already growing in containers such as rigid or flexible plastic pots. Although the sizes vary considerably from an alpine to a shrub, the technique is basically the same. With most types of soil, especially heavy clay, you should add plenty of coarse grit to the bottom of the hole when planting plants such as alpines that prefer dry conditions, as good drainage is essential and they are likely to rot if the soil becomes waterlogged in winter. In light, sandy soils, they should be happy, but you will need to make sure they are watered regularly until established.

PLANTING A MOISTURE-LOVER

When planting moisture-loving plants, remember to leave enough room for larger plants such as *Gunnera* and *Rheum*.

Dig out a hole that is large enough to accommodate the roots. Plant the young plant in the hole to the same depth as it had been planted before. Spread out the roots in the planting hole and take care not to plant too deeply. Cover the roots with the damp soil surrounding the plant in the bed and firm gently. Water in the plant with a fine rose on a watering can.

PLANTING AN ALPINE

Scrambling alpines can be used to soften and disguise the edge of a pool.

1 Dig a hole slightly larger than the spread of the roots alongside the edge.

2 If the soil is heavy, add a smaller layer of coarse grit to the bottom of the hole.

3 Remove the young alpine from its pot, teasing out a few roots so that they spread more widely into the hole. Spread a

well-drained compost (soil mix) around the roots, taking care not to bury the growing point or stems of the plant. Firm in well as the plant is more likely to establish quickly in dry areas if the soil is in firm contact with the roots. Water well and keep moist until the plant can support itself. Do not water for too long a period as this discourages the young plant from becoming self-sufficient.

4 Top-dress the plant with a collar of coarse grit for a more finished effect.

PROPAGATION TECHNIQUES

Most aquatic plants grow so easily that propagation is more often used to replace the existing stock than to increase the quantity of plants. Rejuvenating through propagation is important for containerized plants such as waterlilies and marginals, which quickly use up the nutrients in their compost and become overcrowded, when they are susceptible to pests and diseases.

BY RUNNERS AND OFFSETS

Removing runners from parent plants is an easy method of propagating floating plants. Simply snap off a plantlet when the parent is in full growth in summer. Place the parent and offset back in the pool, where the young plant will need no special care as it has its own root system.

BY WINTER BUDS

Most floating and some submerged plants develop special overwintering buds, known as turions, at the tips of the shoots. These can be simply removed and rooted, providing another method of propagation. The

buds usually form in mid-autumn, when they should be cut off and dibbled into a small container full of aquatic compost (soil mix). When growth begins the following spring, each one can be potted up individually and placed on the pool bottom.

FROM SEED

Propagating by seed is seldom practised because most of the plants are more easily divided. The main exceptions are plants that are treated as annuals, such as bachelor's buttons (*Cotula coronopifolia*), and a few deep-rooted plants with thick rootstocks that are difficult to split, such as skunk cabbage (*Lysichiton*).

Because the seed of aquatic plants tends to lose its viability quickly if it is allowed to dry out, it should be sown as soon as it is ripe in summer or early autumn. Seed of submerged plants and deep-water plants, such as waterlilies, should be sown onto a layer of compost (soil mix) about 8cm (3in) deep in a washing-up bowl or seed pan, then lightly covered with 3mm (⅛in) of

finely sieved aquatic compost (soil mix). Water the compost with a fine rose until the water level covers the compost by 2.5cm (1in). For marginal seeds, the compost can be slightly deeper and 2.5cm (1in) of water should be placed in the bowl so that the seed tray is only just submerged.

Place the container in a frost-free greenhouse and replenish the water regularly to maintain the same level as at sowing. When the seedlings are large enough to handle, prick them out into 8cm (3in) pots of aquatic compost and return to the washing-up bowl. Keep the water covering the pots at the same level as before and grow on until they are large enough to be transferred to a small aquatic planting crate.

LEFT: **Species of *Iris* can be propagated by division, either of the rhizome or offsets, in late summer or by seed in autumn. Named cultivars should be propagated by division only.**

ABOVE: **The delicate pink flowers of pink or thrift (*Armeria maritima*), an evergreen, clump-forming perennial, appear in summer. It can be propagated by seed in the autumn.**

PROPAGATING FROM SEED

For most aquatic plants, it is generally best to sow seed as soon as it has been gathered so that it is fresh. Propagation from seed is a perfect way of obtaining large quantities of any one plant if you are planning to plant large areas. The best time to collect seed from the plant is just as it begins to disperse the seed naturally. The following sequence is especially suitable for marginal plants.

1 Fill a seed pan to the brim with aquatic compost (soil mix).

2 Firm the compost (soil mix) thoroughly using a square, flat piece of wood which will ensure that the corners are adequately compressed.

3 Sow the seeds evenly across the surface of the compost (soil mix), leaving a small gap between each seed.

4 Using a fine sieve, cover the seed with a shallow covering of sieved compost (soil mix), using just enough compost to cover the seed.

5 Using a fine rose on a watering can, water the compost (soil mix) thoroughly and evenly.

6 After watering, place the seed pan in a watertight container. For the seed of marginal plants, pour approximately 2.5cm (1in) of water into the surrounding container so that the seed tray containing the seeds is only just submerged. Maintain this water level in the container and no further watering should be necessary on the surface of the compost (soil mix). If the seed is from a submerged plant or a deep-water aquatic, such as a waterlily, then submerge the seed pan in 2.5cm (1in) of water. Use fine sharp sand on the compost surface to prevent particles of soil floating in the water.

SOFTWOOD CUTTINGS

Oxygenating plants are propagated by taking cuttings. They produce masses of young, soft growth in summer, and this can be cut off into pieces 15–23cm (6–9in) long. Bunch the shoots together and bind them with florist's wire near the base before inserting them into small aquatic baskets full of aquatic compost (soil mix). Top-dress with pea gravel, and then submerge the baskets.

TAKING SOFTWOOD CUTTINGS

This is a very simple method of propagating aquatics, from submerged oxygenating plants to several of the marginals that make soft sappy growth in the summer.

1 Remove a young shoot approximately 15-23cm (6-9in) long from the parent plant and make a cut with a sharp knife just underneath a leaf joint on the stem to leave one cutting of about 15cm (6in) long.

2 Using a sharp knife, trim off the young leaves at the base as close as possible to the stem.

3 Having filled a small container with fine-mesh sides with aquatic compost (soil mix), make a hole in the centre of the compost deep enough for the base of the cutting to be inserted securely.

4 Firm the compost (soil mix) around the cutting to make the stem more secure.

5 Top-dress the compost (soil mix) with washed pea shingle or gravel to prevent particles of soil from floating to the surface. Water the plant thoroughly with a fine rose on a watering can. If it is a submerged plant, the cutting can be placed under water immediately. If it is a marginal plant, then partially submerge the container in water 5cm (2in) deep and spray the cutting regularly with a fine mist spray until it has rooted. Keep the cuttings indoors out of direct sunlight, preferably inside a large, clear plastic bag. Remove this daily and spray the plants with a fine mist until they have rooted. If possible, store in a cool greenhouse while the cutting is taking root.

DIVIDING WATERLILIES AND DEEP-WATER PLANTS

Division is by far the most common method of propagation, and it simply consists of splitting the root system into two or more parts with a sharp knife, a spade or two forks placed back to back so that the roots are prized apart.

Waterlilies will soon become overgrown in containers, and will often develop roots outside the container. Overgrown plants tend to make leaves at the expense of producing flowers. If the leaves start to stick out of the water, then the waterlily is in need of dividing.

For plants such as waterlilies, which have thick roots, division involves cutting the root into sections so that each piece has a growing bud. You will need to lift the waterlily rootstock out of the pond and clean it thoroughly first by hosing it down. Remove the old leaves and cut the plump sections of the waterlily root-stock into sections, approximately 5–8cm (2–3in) in length. Make sure that each section of the rootstock has new growth at its tip. Trim back the thin roots on the underside of the rootstock.

Fill a small basket with aquatic compost (soil mix) and firm in thoroughly. Press the piece of young root onto the compost so that the growing tip is above the surface and at the same angle as it was in the water. Top-dress with 2.5cm (1in) of pea shingle or gravel and water in thoroughly. After the division has been planted, the basket is submerged in the water so that the growing point is covered by no more than 5–8cm (2–3in) of water.

Some types of waterlily form tuberous roots, and it is possible to cut off individual side shoots flush to the tuber. The species *Nymphaea tuberosa* develops small nodes on the tuber, and these can be snapped off and planted individually. Any exposed or cut surfaces should be dusted with charcoal before pressing them firmly onto the aquatic compost (soil mix) and treating them as the rhizomatous waterlilies.

DIVIDING A WATERLILY

When the leaves of waterlilies start to stick out of the water, this is an indication that the plant needs dividing.

1 Cut off the end of the rootstock which contains the growing point. Cut off the smaller, thin feeding roots from the thick rhizome as close to the rhizome as possible.

2 Further reduce the rhizome to no more than 5–8cm (2–3in) long, making a clean cut with a sharp knife.

3 Cut off the leaves and flowers at the base of their stems, leaving no more than 2–3 young developing leaves.

4 Fill a large, fine-mesh container nearly to the rim with aquatic compost (soil mix) and firm in well.

5 Firm the young stem into the surface of the compost (soil mix) and position it so that the growing point is directed away from the corner of the container.

6 Top-dress with pea shingle before submerging the container in the pool.

DIVIDING MARGINALS

Many marginal plants are propagated easily by division, and vigorous plants in small containers will benefit from this procedure on an annual basis. You will need to remove the plant from the pond first of all in order to assess how potbound the specimen is and whether there is a suitable point to make the division.

To divide a marginal, discard the older inner pieces and select the more vigorous and younger outer portions. Pot these up into a container of aquatic compost (soil mix), planting at the same depth as before, and immerse in water so that the water just covers the crown. Cut back aerial shoots to within 5cm (2in) of the water level.

There are slightly different methods for dividing marginal plants, depending on whether they are clump-forming, fibrous-rooted or have thick rhizomatous roots.

DIVIDING A CLUMP-ROOTED MARGINAL

Several marginals are clump-forming in habit. Clump-forming plants tend to form clumps with several crowns or growing points, which are clustered together. This differs from other common types of marginal which form thick rhizomatous roots, with the buds and growing points distributed along the length of the root.

If the plant is not too old, the clump can be teased apart by gently pulling the roots between thumb and finger. In older or more vigorous plants, it is often necessary to break up the crown with a hand fork, or, if this is still not strong enough, the pieces may need cutting apart with a knife.

1 Vigorous marginals that are grown in small containers should be divided annually. Remove the plant from the pond

and assess how potbound it is. This is also the time to check whether there is a suitable point to make the division.

2 After removing from the container, tease the leaves apart and cut through the roots on the outside of the clump with a large knife.

3 Having removed a young portion of the plant with healthy leaves and a growing point, half-fill the original container with fresh aquatic compost (soil mix).

4 Place the young piece of the divided plant into the container and add more compost (soil mix) to bury the roots. Firm as much compost as possible into the container.

5 Top-dress the compost (soil mix) with pea shingle or gravel before putting the plant back into the pool. This top-dressing ensures that the particles of soil do not escape into the water.

DIVIDING A FIBROUS-ROOTED MARGINAL

Fibrous-rooted aquatics are less common than fibrous-rooted terrestrial plants. This is because the fibrous root system is more suited to dry soils. However, there are some aquatics with fibrous root systems, and these can be propagated through division.

1 Tease out the stems and roots that have become intertwined. Spread the roots out on a flat surface and cut through a portion of the young growth at the edge which has growing points and healthy leaves.

2 Fill a medium-size, fine-mesh container with aquatic compost (soil mix) to about half full.

3 Place the young portion of the divided plant into the container and cover the roots with compost (soil mix).

4 Firm in the newly divided plant well so that the compost is fairly compact.

5 Top-dress with pea shingle or gravel to ensure that the compost (soil mix) does not escape when the basket is submerged.

DIVIDING A MARGINAL WITH THICK RHIZOMATOUS ROOTS

Many marginal aquatics have thick, hard rhizomatous roots which grow in a straight line on the surface of the mud. This type of root system is quite common among marginal plants, notably the many species of *Iris* that prefer their roots on the surface of the mud.

1 Remove the younger pieces of rhizomatous root which contain 2–3 leaves.

2 Cut up the root so that each piece contains a leaf.

3 Trim off the fibrous roots on the underside of the rhizome to within 2.5cm (1in).

ABOVE: *Iris pseudacorus* var. *bastardii* is a rhizomatous iris with lovely, soft yellow flowers. It can be propagated by division.

RIGHT: *Iris versicolor* is a rhizomatous iris which can be easily propagated by division.

4 Fill a small container that has fine-mesh sides with aquatic compost (soil mix) to the rim of the container.

5 After firming the compost (soil mix) in the container, make a small depression in the compost (soil mix) with a dibber (dibble) to enable the rhizome to be half buried in the depression.

6 Firm the root thoroughly into the depression on the compost so that the cutting is stable. It is also important to firm the compost (soil mix) in very well in order to minimize the reduction in volume which can occur when the basket is placed in the pool, and large amounts of air are expelled from the compost.

7 Top-dress the compost (soil mix) with washed pea shingle or gravel to increase the stability of the young division and prevent compost floating to the surface. Place in shallow water to the depth of the container in a shaded position until it develops enough roots to survive in strong sun, and then place on the marginal shelf.

A garden using both water and rock involves almost opposite ends of the cultivation spectrum. Alpines are suited

PLANT DIRECTORY

to the dry soil along some pool edges, but most of this section covers aquatic plants. The growth of most temperate aquatics can be restrained by a basket, but care is required for exotic plants as they can get out of control.

OPPOSITE: **A massed planting of candelabra primulas looks spectacular in the moist soil by the side of a pond.**

FREE-FLOATING PLANTS

It is particularly important to introduce floating plants when you are establishing a new pond. These plants not only reduce algae by cutting down light and absorbing mineral salts through their suspended roots, but also provide valuable homes for fish fry. The reduction of surface light is an important part of the planting strategy, although totally covering the water's surface would do more harm than good by blocking out too much

energy-giving light. Between one-half and two-thirds of the surface area should be covered by the leaves of either surface floaters or waterlilies. This cover is difficult to achieve on a new pond and you may have to resort to using more floaters than will ultimately be necessary and later netting off when the pond becomes more established. A selection of the more common and widely available floaters is given here.

Azolla (Azollaceae)
Mosquito fern, water fern, fairy moss
The genus contains eight species of dainty, green, floating plants. They quickly reproduce by division, and their rapid rate of reproduction means they should be netted off a small pond as soon as they swamp the surface.
Propagation: By division.
Hardiness: Half hardy to frost tender.

Azolla filiculoides (syn. *A. caroliniana*)
This small, perennial, half hardy fern forms clusters of soft, pale green fronds, 1–5cm (½–2in) long, which turn purplish-red in autumn. Each leaf is attached to a single fine root. It can be invasive, so thin regularly. It survives cold winters by producing overwintering bodies, which sink to the bottom of the pool, but resurface when the water warms up in late spring.
Cultivation: Grow in full sun.
Height: To 5cm (2in); *spread:* indefinite.

Eichhornia (Pontederiaceae)
Water hyacinth, water orchid
There are seven species in this genus of tropical, mainly floating plants

Azolla filiculoides

from South America, where they root into any shallow mud and form huge colonies, which can swamp rivers and lakes, becoming a major problem.
Propagation: By breaking off young offsets, which is very easily done.
Hardiness: Borderline hardy.

Eichhornia crassipes (syn. *E. speciosa*)
Water hyacinth
This tender plant will not survive winter outdoors in temperate climates. It is available in summer and for a few months in hot weather provides a striking sight on the pool surface. It bears rosettes of shiny, pale green leaves, the swollen, spongy bases of which act as floats. In very warm summers it produces pale blue, hyacinth-like flowers to 15–23cm (6–9in) high. Long, feathery roots, purplish-black in colour, provide a perfect medium for spawning goldfish. It spreads by means of fast-growing stolons, and in some countries with warm climates is prohibited because it chokes waterways. This is not a problem in temperate climates, and it will only be successful in areas with sunny, warm weather. Overwinter in a frost-free greenhouse on trays of moist soil.

Cultivation: Grow in full sun and warm water, preferably 18°C (64°F).
Height: 15–23cm (6–9in); *spread:* 15–30cm (6–12in).

Hydrocharis (Hydrocharitaceae)
Frogbit
The two species of submerged or free-floating plants in this genus are native to temperate and subtropical parts of Europe, Africa, Asia and Australia. These plants have short, stolon-like stems, which form mats just under the surface of the water.
Propagation: By removing offsets, which is easily done.
Hardiness: Hardy.

Hydrocharis morsus-ranae
Frogbit
Rather like a tiny waterlily, this graceful little floater has kidney-shaped, shiny green leaves, 3cm (1¼in) long, in a rosette and small white flowers which have a yellow centre.
Cultivation: Grow in full sun in water to 30cm (12in) deep.
Spread: Indefinite.

Eichhornia crassipes

Lemna (Lemnaceae)
Duckweed, frog's buttons
The genus contains 13 species of small, temperate and tropical floating plants, found in almost all parts of the world. They form green floating mats in still or slow-moving water. The flowers are small and have no decorative merit.
Propagation: By removing young plants.
Hardiness: Hardy to half hardy.

Lemna minor
Lesser duckweed
This is the most widespread of all the duckweeds. It has light green, ovate leaves, about 5mm (¼in) across, with a single rootlet hanging down from each one. It is a valuable food for goldfish.
Cultivation: Grow in full sun or shade.
Spread: Indefinite.

Lemna trisulca
Star duckweed, ivy-leaved duckweed
This species is the easiest to control because it reproduces more slowly than the other duckweeds. The light green, almost transparent leaves are elliptical in shape, about 1cm (½in) across, with the young plants growing at right angles to the old ones.
Cultivation: Grow in sun or shade.
Spread: Indefinite.

Hydrocharis morsus-ranae

Pistia stratiotes

Stratiotes aloides

Trapa natans

Pistia (Araceae)

Water lettuce, shell flower
There is only one species in this genus. It is a floating plant, which is found growing throughout the world in tropical and subtropical areas. It produces rosettes of leaves, which resemble those of lettuces. Radiating stolons terminate in new plantlets, each in turn producing further plantlets, which result in this plant being a nuisance in warm tropical waters.
Propagation: By removing the young plantlets.
Hardiness: Frost tender.

Pistia stratiotes

A deciduous, perennial, floating aquatic, this species is evergreen in tropical waters which are warmer than 19–21°C (66–70°F). The slightly overlapping, wedge-shaped, velvety, sessile leaves grow to approximately 25cm (10in) in length and are 10cm (4in) wide. They have crenated tips and are a soft shade of pale green on the upper side and whitish green on the underside. The tiny greenish flowers are produced at various times in leaflike spathes in the leaf axils.
Cultivation: Grow in warm water, with a minimum temperature of 10–15°C (50–59°F), in full sun.
Height: 10cm (4in); *spread*: indefinite.

Salvinia (Salviniaceae)

This is a cosmopolitan genus of ten species of free-floating aquatic ferns, which are found in tropical and subtropical areas. Some species can be grown in temperate regions, where they have become naturalized. Second only to the water hyacinth in its rate of growth, the plants have become a pest in southeastern Africa and southern India. The floating leaves are soft to the touch and have a covering of silky hairs.
Propagation: By separating the stems in spring or summer.
Hardiness: Half hardy.

Salvinia natans

This attractive species bears roundish, green leaflets, up to 2.5cm (1in) long, which have shiny brown hairs on the underside. The plant also has a submerged, root-like frond.
Cultivation: Grow in full sun in water with a minimum temperature of 10°C (50°F).
Height: 2.5cm (1in); *spread*: indefinite.

Stratiotes (Hydrocharitaceae)

Water soldier, water aloe
The single species in this genus is a semi-submerged or floating aquatic plant that is native to Europe and northwestern Asia. The sword-like leaves resemble pineapple tops.
Propagation: By separating runners from the parent plant.
Hardiness: Hardy.

Stratiotes aloides

This semi-evergreen, perennial floater can form quite extensive stands of prickly rosettes on the surface of the water. These are formed by long, olive-green leaves, approximately 50cm (20in) long and 2cm (¾in) wide, with serrated edges. The tips of the leaves frequently emerge above the water's surface. In summer the whole plant tries to surface in order to produce cup-shaped, white, sometimes pink-tinged flowers about 4cm (1½in) across.
Cultivation: Grow in water to 1m (3ft) deep and in sun so that it will produce flowers.
Height: 40cm (16in); *spread*: indefinite.

Trapa (Trapaceae)

Water chestnut
There are 15 species of temperate and subtropical floaters in this genus. All species within this genus colonize shallow, still water. This plant is rich in fat and starch, and for this reason the plants are eaten in continental Asia, Malaysia and India.
Propagation: By seed sown in spring.
Hardiness: Frost hardy to frost tender.

Trapa natans

Jesuit's nut, water caltrop
An annual floating plant, this frost hardy species forms rosettes of pale green, glossy, diamond-shaped leaves, 2.5cm (1in) across, with conspicuous veins and serrated edges. The leaves are carried on long, reddish, inflated petioles. The inconspicuous white flowers produce fruits like thorny black chestnuts, 5cm (2in) in diameter, with four spikes.
Cultivation: Grow in full sun in water with a minimum temperature of 10°C (50°F).
Spread: Indefinite.

Lemna minor

Salvinia natans

OXYGENATING PLANTS

Oxygenators are the first group to be planted in a new pool. They are sold in bunches of unrooted stems, about 23cm (9in) long, nipped together at the base by a piece of lead. The weight prevents them from floating to the surface if they are loosened after planting. They are available throughout summer, and in a new pool it is best to give them a start by planting them into crates on the bottom. In an established pool, however, where some mud will have accumulated on the bottom, they can simply be weighted down and dropped into the pool over as wide an area as possible. They should not be planted deeper than 1–1.2m (3–4ft) deep, and they do best at depths between 45–60cm (18–24in). A medium-size planting crate will hold five or six bunches of oxygenators, and in general this planted crate will be adequate for 1 square metre of surface area; this is equivalent to one bunch to each square foot of surface area.

Callitriche
(Callitrichaceae)
Water starwort
The 25 species in this genus are distributed throughout the world, except South Africa. They are small, slender plants, and they generally grow in a tight mass in a wide range of habitats, but mainly in temperate locations. Most species are recognizable by their terminal rosettes of leaves, which, when floating on the water, give rise to the common name.
Propagation: By softwood cuttings.
Hardiness: Hardy.

Callitriche hermaphroditica (syn. *C. autumnalis*)
Autumn starwort
This hardy species has light green, linear leaves, 1–2cm (½–¾in) long, held opposite each other on thin, branching stems, to 50cm (20in) long. The mass of stems provides homes for minute life, while the young leaves are a delicacy for goldfish. This species is the exception to the rule in not forming rosettes of floating leaves.
Cultivation: Grow in sun or partial shade in water to 50cm (20in) deep.
Spread: Indefinite.

Ceratophyllum demersum

Ceratophyllum
(Ceratophyllaceae)
The genus contains about 30 hardy species of submerged rootless aquatics, found around the world. They grow only in submerged conditions and are unable to tolerate even the shortest time out of water. They flourish in cold water and shade, conditions that could inhibit other species.

Propagation: By detaching small pieces of stem and floating them in the water.
Hardiness: Hardy to frost tender.

Ceratophyllum demersum
Hornwort
The leaves usually form clusters 30–60cm (1–2ft) long. The whorls of slender, rather brittle, forked, dark green leaves, 1–4cm (½–1½in) long, crowd towards the apex. Hornwort is hardy, and useful in more shaded ponds. It is often found free-floating or loosely anchored in the bottom mud in both still and moving water. It has inconspicuous flowers, which are borne in the leaf axils. To overwinter, the tips of the shoots shorten and thicken and then break off before sinking to the bottom. *C. submersum* is slightly more vigorous, with stems reaching nearly 1m (3ft) and leaves growing to 2.5–5cm (1–2in) in length.
Cultivation: Grow in sun or shade in water to 1m (3ft) deep.
Spread: Indefinite.

Egeria
(Hydrocharitaceae)
The two species of evergreen or semi-evergreen submerged plants in this genus were originally native to the warm and temperate zones of South America, but they have become established elsewhere, sometimes becoming so invasive that they are regarded as pests.
Propagation: By softwood cuttings.
Hardiness: Hardy to frost tender.

Egeria densa (syn. *Elodea densa*)
Argentinian water weed
This frost-tender species has long, branching stems, to 1m (3ft) long, with whorls of narrow, dark green leaves, each 2.5cm (1in) long and with a pointed tip that usually curls backwards. Plants may produce insignificant white flowers on the surface of the water in summer.
Cultivation: Grow in full sun.
Spread: Indefinite.

Hottonia
(Primulaceae)
The genus contains two species of submerged plants which have primula-like flowers, held above the water. The two species are mainly found in bright, clear pools or slow-moving ditches in temperate areas of the northern hemisphere.
Propagation: By seed or by division.
Hardiness: Hardy to half hardy.

Callitriche hermaphroditica

Hottonia palustris

Ceratophyllum submersum

Hottonia palustris

Water violet

In summer, the fully hardy water violet bears beautiful spikes of violet flowers, which have yellow throats. The flower spikes are held well above the surface of the water on stalks that grow to 30–40cm (12–16in) tall. The submerged, bright green leaves are finely divided and reach a length of 2–13cm (¾–5in). They are arranged in an attractive, comb-like fashion.

Cultivation: Grow in full sun and clear water.

Height: 1m (3ft); *spread:* indefinite.

Lagarosiphon

(Hydrocharitaceae)

Curly water thyme

There are nine species of tender, submerged plants in this genus. They are native to central Africa and Madagascar, but they have also established themselves in Europe and New Zealand. Similar to *Egeria*, curly water thyme is an excellent oxygenator for fish bowls, pools and aquaria.

Propagation: By softwood cuttings, which is easily done.

Hardiness: Hardy to half hardy.

Lagarosiphon major
(syn. Elodea crispa)

This hardy, semi-evergreen perennial has narrow, strongly recurved, fresh green leaves, 5–25mm (¼–1in) long, borne in spirals along the stem. The dense masses of submerged stems should be cut back every autumn.

Cultivation: Grow in full sun.

Height and spread: 1m (3ft).

Myriophyllum aquaticum

Myriophyllum
(Haloragaceae)

Milfoil

The 40 species of submerged aquatics in this genus are mainly from the southern hemisphere. The submerged stems are often long, bearing finely divided, almost feathery leaves, which are extremely attractive. The milfoils show a great diversity of habit, and many love to creep out of the water and scramble onto the surrounds of the pool.

Propagation: By softwood cuttings, which is easily done.

Hardiness: Hardy to frost hardy.

Myriophyllum aquaticum
(syn. M. brasiliense, M. proserpinacoides)

Diamond milfoil, parrot's feather

This species is slightly tender and must be well submerged in temperate climates if it is to survive the winter. It is, nevertheless, extensively used in outdoor pools, where the graceful foliage and stems take root in the wet soil above the water line. The stems can grow to 50cm–1.5m (20–60in) long, with leaves 2.5–5cm (1–2in) long and borne in whorls of four to six, divided into four to eight bright green segments.

Cultivation: Grow in sun or partial shade and thin clumps regularly.

Spread: Indefinite.

Potamogeton
(Potamogetonaceae)

There are 80–100 species of submerged aquatic plants in this genus, and they are found in temperate regions throughout the world. They are vigorous rhizomatous perennials, and only a few are suitable as oxygenators in decorative ponds as they can quickly choke other growth.

Propagation: By stem cuttings in early summer.

Hardiness: Hardy to frost tender.

Potamogeton crispus

Curled pondweed

The stems of this hardy species can grow to 4m (13ft) or more, and bear narrow, stalkless leaves, each about 8cm (3in) long and 5–10mm (¼–⅜in) wide. They are almost translucent, with wavy edges, and vary from green to reddish-brown.

Cultivation: Grow in full sun if possible, but it tolerates cloudy water better than any other oxygenator.

Spread: Indefinite.

Ranunculus
(Ranunculaceae)

This large genus contains about 400 species of temperate and tropical moisture-loving and aquatic species, which have a big impact in the garden.

Propagation: By softwood cuttings for the submerged species.

Hardiness: Hardy.

Ranunculus aquatilis

Water crowfoot

This hardy, submerged, clump-forming perennial bears flat, kidney-shaped, floating leaves, 3–8cm (1½–3in) long, and threadlike, submerged leaves. The buttercup-shaped, white flowers, held above the water, are 2cm (¾in) across with a yellow base to the petals.

Cultivation: Grow in full sun in water to 1m (3ft) deep at a depth of 15–60cm (6–24in), where it can root in the mud.

Spread: Indefinite.

Ranunculus aquatilis

DEEP-WATER PLANTS

There are a few species of water plants that prefer deeper water than the marginals and that will grow in the same conditions as waterlilies. They are usually grouped in a section called deep-water plants in aquatic catalogues; although it is not a large category, these plants make a valuable contribution to the appearance of the pool in providing a welcome change in shape from the pads of waterlilies when you are selecting the surface leaves. As well as being decorative, their leaves also provide valuable shade.

Aponogeton
(Aponogetonaceae)
The genus contains some 44 species of rhizomatous perennials, which are found in mainly tropical and subtropical areas, but there is one hardy species, which is used extensively in cold-water ponds.
Propagation: The hardy species is propagated by seed or by dividing the rhizomes into sections with a bud.
Hardiness: Hardy to frost tender.

Aponogeton distachyos
Water hawthorn, Cape pondweed
This frost-hardy perennial aquatic has oblong, bright green leaves, to 20cm (8in) long by 8cm (3in) wide, which can become almost evergreen in mild winters. The strongly scented flowers are often produced in two flushes, the main flush in spring and a second as a most welcome surprise in the autumn. The beautiful white flowers, which have purple-brown anthers, are 10cm (4in) long and are held above the water. A very tolerant plant, particularly of shade, it extends the flowering season, and its long leaves add interest to the water surface.
Cultivation: Grow in sun or shade in water to 60cm (2ft).
Spread: 1.2m (4ft).

Euryale (Nymphaeaceae)
Fox nuts, Gorgon plant
The genus contains a single species of large aquatic plants, which are native to India, Bangladesh and China. The floating leaves are spiny, and this has given rise to the common name Gorgon plant, a reference to the mythological snake-haired Gorgon.
Propagation: By seed.
Hardiness: Frost tender.

Euryale ferox
This is a spectacular plant. The large, puckered leaves, 60cm–1m (2–3ft) in diameter, have prominent veins and spines. The flowers are relatively small – 5cm (2in) across – for such a large-leaved plant. They are violet-magenta in colour and mature to a berry containing seeds the size of a pea.
Cultivation: Grow in full sun in water about 1m (3ft) deep and with a minimum temperature of 5°C (41°F).
Spread: 1.5m (5ft).

Nuphar (Nymphaeaceae)
Cow lily, spatterdock
There are 25 species of aquatics in the genus, and they are found in temperate areas of the northern hemisphere. They bear some resemblance to waterlilies but have tougher floating leaves and will grow in conditions that are either too deep or too shaded for waterlilies.
Propagation: By division of the rhizome during summer.
Hardiness: Hardy to frost hardy.

Nuphar japonica
Japanese pond lily
This hardy species is much smaller than the other nuphars. It has wavy, heart-shaped, submerged leaves, which are a delicate purplish colour, and dark green, oblong, surface leaves, with arrow-shaped bases, 40cm (16in) long. The red-tinted yellow flowers are 5cm (2in) across.
Cultivation: Grow in full sun in water 30–60cm (1–2ft) deep.
Spread: 1m (3ft).

Aponogeton distachyos

Nuphar lutea

Nuphar lutea

Yellow pond lily
A common hardy species, this nuphar survives in deep and slow-moving water. The leathery floating leaves are 40cm (16in) long, and the bowl-shaped yellow flowers are 5cm (2in) across.
Cultivation: Grow in sun or partial shade in water 30–60cm (1–2ft) deep.
Spread: 2m (6½ft).

Nymphoides
(Menyanthaceae)
Floating heart
There are 20 species of submerged aquatics in this genus. They originate from temperate and subtropical areas around the world, and they resemble miniature waterlilies. They are often found in shallow, still waters, spreading very quickly to form a carpet of leaves.
Propagation: By dividing the long, thin roots in early spring.
Hardiness: Hardy to frost tender.

Nymphoides peltata

Yellow floating heart,
water fringe
This hardy species spreads rapidly by means of the extensive runners that carry the small, heart-shaped leaves, which are about 5cm (2in) across. The leaves are often mottled and splashed with brown. The yellow flowers, 2cm (¾in) in diameter, are fringed and held just above the water; they appear in summer.
Cultivation: Grow in full sun in water no deeper than 45cm (18in).
Spread: Indefinite.

Victoria amazonica

Victoria (Nymphaeaceae)
Giant waterlily, water platter
The genus contains two species of tropical aquatics with very large floating leaves. The species are native to tropical America.
Propagation: By seed.
Hardiness: Frost tender.

Victoria amazonica

Amazon waterlily, royal water lily
The rounded, floating leaves can reach up to 1.8m (6ft) across and are reddish-purple underneath. The leaves are covered with large prickles and the rims are vertical. The white, waterlily-like flowers appear in summer.
Cultivation: Grow in full sun in water 1m (3ft) deep and with a minimum temperature of 25°C (77°F).
Spread: 6m (20ft).

Victoria 'Longwood'

This cultivar was raised at Longwood Gardens in Philadelphia in the United States. It is an amazing plant, with a very fast rate of growth, quickly developing enormous, circular, floating, glossy green leaves. These can grow to 1.2–1.8m (4–6ft) in diameter, with upturned rims. The large nocturnal flowers, 25–40cm (10–16in) in diameter, last only two nights, and they turn from white to pink then purplish-red.
Cultivation: Grow in full sun in water 1m (3ft) deep and with a minimum temperature of 22°C (72°F).
Spread (in a single season): 7m (23ft).

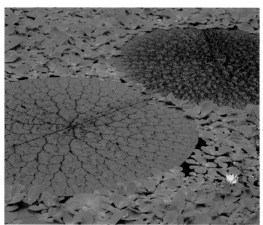

Euryale ferox

Nymphoides peltata

WATERLILIES

In addition to the grouping of waterlilies (*Nymphaea*) by colour, the following are further subdivided into hardy and tropical plants. All the hardy types will succeed without protection in temperate regions outdoors; the tropical plants, on the other hand, will need to be grown in a sunny glasshouse in all but the most favoured locations.

The flowers vary in size, but they are generally always in proportion to the leaf, ranging from 2.5cm (1in) across in the pygmy varieties, to 30cm (1ft) across in some of the tropicals. There are waterlilies suitable for every

size of pond, from barrels and tubs to extensive pools. All should be given a sunny, sheltered position without any water turbulence on their leaves. The planting depth given here refers to the depth of water above the crown or growing point and not to the depth of pond. The spread refers to the average area that the leaves will eventually cover, although in small planting containers they may not achieve these sizes. This selection includes species and cultivars that should be commercially available, although the tropical types are less easy to source in temperate areas.

PINK
Hardy waterlilies

Nymphaea 'Amabilis'
The star-shaped flowers, which grow to approximately 15–19cm (6–7½in) across, have pink petals with lighter tips surrounding deep yellow stamens. The nearly round leaves are green, 24cm (9½in) in diameter and reddish-purple when young.
Approximate spread: 1.5–2.3m (5–7½ft).
Suggested planting depth: 30–45cm (12–18in).

Nymphaea 'American Star'
The star-like flowers, which grow to about 15–18cm (6–7in) in diameter, have pink petals with light tips surrounding deep yellow stamens. The young leaves are reddish-purple, turning green as they mature. They are round in shape and 25–28cm (10–11in) across.
Approximate spread: 1.2–1.5m (4–5ft).
Suggested planting depth: 30–45cm (12–18in).

Nymphaea 'Comanche'

Nymphaea 'Attraction'
Cup-like, later star-shaped, pink flowers are 15–20cm (6–8in) across with slightly lighter outer petals and glowing orange stamens. The oval leaves are 25–30cm (10–12in) long, light bronze when young, turning mid green with age. One of the best pinks for cut flowers although the central petals can "burn" on hot days.
Approximate spread: 1.2–1.5m (4–5ft).
Suggested planting depth: 30–45cm (12–18in).

Nymphaea 'Caroliniana Perfecta'

Nymphaea 'Caroliniana Perfecta'
The cup-like, salmon-pink flowers of this waterlily are approximately 13–15cm (5–6in) across and have a sweet scent. The leaves are nearly round, 23–25cm (9–10in) across, bronzy at first, turning dark green with reddish brown undersides.
Approximate spread: 1.2–1.5m (4–5ft).
Suggested planting depth: 30–45cm (12–18in).

Nymphaea 'Comanche'
The cup-like, later stellate, flowers are 13–15cm (5–6in) across. They change from yellow apricot to gold orange, flushed with pink, then finally to deep orange, flushed with red. The stamens are yellow. The leaves are nearly round, 30cm (12in) across, bronzy when young with a few purple flecks. This is the largest and one of the showiest of the changeable cultivars.
Approximate spread: 1.2–1.5m (4–5ft).
Suggested planting depth: 30–45cm (12–18in).

Nymphaea 'Darwin' (syn. N. 'Hollandia')
The double, peony-style flowers, 15–19cm (6–7½in) across, have light pink inner petals and lighter pink, almost white outer petals surrounding pinkish-yellow stamens. The new leaves are brownish, turning green as they mature. They are round in shape and 25–28cm (10–11in) across.
Approximate spread: 1.2–1.5m (4–5ft).
Suggested planting depth: 30–60cm (1–2ft).

Nymphaea 'Attraction'

Nymphaea 'Laydekeri Lilacea'

Nymphaea 'Fabiola' (syn. *N.* 'Mrs Richmond')

The peony-shaped flowers, 15–18cm (6–7in) across, have pinkish-red, highly flecked petals surrounding orange stamens. The longish leaves, 30cm (12in) long, turn from bronzy purple to green.
Approximate spread: 1.5m (5ft).
Suggested planting depth: 30cm (12in).

Nymphaea 'Firecrest'

The star-shaped flowers, 14–15cm (5½–6in) across, have lavender pink petals surrounding orange and pink stamens. The round leaves, 23cm (9in) in diameter, change from deep purple when young to green.
Approximate spread: 1.2m (4ft).
Suggested planting depth: 23–30cm (9–12in).

Nymphaea 'Laydekeri Lilacea'

The cup-like, lilac-pink flowers are 6–9cm (2½–3½in) across with deep yellow stamens. The leaves are nearly round, 18–20cm (7–8in) across, purplish when young, turning olive-green with a few purple mottles.
Approximate spread: 1–1.2m (3–4ft).
Suggested planting depth: 15cm (6in).

Nymphaea 'Marliacea Carnea' (syn. *N.* 'Apple Blossom Pink')

The cup-shaped, light pink flowers, 12–13cm (4.5–5in) across, have yellow stamens. Purplish when young, the mature leaves are oval, deep green, and 19–20cm (7½–8in) long.
Approximate spread: 1.2–1.5m (4–5ft).
Suggested planting depth: 30–45cm (12–18in).

Nymphaea 'Pink Sensation'

Nymphaea 'Mrs. George C. Hitchcock'

A night-blooming cultivar which holds its large, soft-rose flowers, 25–28cm (10–11in) across, well above the water where the dark orange stamens are seen to good effect. The wavy, copper-green leaves, which are 38cm by 34cm (15in by 13½in), are flecked with darker green on the upper side and purplish brown beneath. This is a very reliable waterlily which flowers well into autumn.
Approximate spread: 2.2–2.4m (7–8ft).
Suggested planting depth: 45cm (18in).

Nymphaea 'Odorata Turicensis'

The fragrant, star-shaped flowers, 13–15cm (5–6in) across, have lovely soft pink petals surrounding deep yellow stamens. The round, green leaves are 13–15cm (5–6in) across and have bronzy red undersides.
Approximate spread: 2.4m (8ft).
Suggested planting depth: 23–30cm (9–12in).

Nymphaea 'Perry's Pink'

The star-shaped flowers, 15–18cm (6–7in) across, have rich pink petals and yellow to orange stamens. There is an unusual red dot in the centre of each flower. The new leaves are reddish-purple, turning green as they mature, and are round in shape, to 28cm (11in) across. Plant in a large container for the best flowering.
Approximate spread: 1.2–1.5m (4–5ft).
Suggested planting depth: 30–60cm (1–2ft).

Nymphaea 'Pink Sensation'

The cup-shaped flowers, which become star-shaped, are 12–15cm (5–6in) across and have pink petals surrounding yellow and pink stamens. Purplish when young, the round leaves mature to green and are up to 25cm (10in) in diameter. This is one of the best pinks, and the flowers stay open late into the afternoon.
Approximate spread: 1.2m (4ft).
Suggested planting depth: 30–45cm (12–18in).

Nymphaea 'Pygmaea Rubra'

The small, cup-like flowers, 6cm (2½in) across, have outer petals that are a white-blushed pink in colour as they open and become rich maroon red later. The stamens are yellow. Bronzy when young, the leaves are round and green when mature, and 15–18cm (6–7in) across.
Approximate spread: 75cm (30in).
Suggested planting depth: 15–23cm (6–9in).

Nymphaea 'Rose Arey'

Nymphaea 'Marliacea Carnea'

Nymphaea 'General Pershing'

Nymphaea 'Ray Davies'

The peony-shaped, almost double flowers, which are 15–18cm (6–7in) across, have yellow and pink petals surrounding yellow stamens. The young leaves are slightly bronzed, later turning to glossy green, and 25–28cm (10–11in) in diameter.
Approximate spread: 1.5m (5ft).
Suggested planting depth: 30cm (12in).

Nymphaea 'Rose Arey'

The star-shaped, sweetly scented flowers are 18–20cm (7–8in) in diameter and have golden stamens. The flowers change towards the margins from pink to orange-pink. The purple young leaves mature to round plain green leaves, 23cm (9in) in diameter.
Approximate spread: 1.2–1.5m (4–5ft).
Suggested planting depth: 38–60cm (15–24in).

Tropical waterlilies

Nymphaea capensis var. zanzibariensis

This is a day-blooming and free-flowering form that has larger flowers than *N. capensis*, reaching 18–25cm (7–10in) across. The hybrid 'Wild Rose' was introduced in 1941 by George Pring who was the famous American breeder of tropical waterlilies. The flowers have an almost bi-colour effect, which is caused by the large pink petals being flushed with yellow at their base and combined with a mass of golden stamens that are tipped with pink. The blooms are held at a height of 20–25cm (8–10in) above the water. The leaves are a dark green, flecked with reddish brown above, and light green, flushed with red, underneath.
Approximate spread: 1.5–2.4m (5–8ft).
Suggested planting depth: 45cm (18in).

Nymphaea 'Froebelii'

Nymphaea 'James Brydon'

Nymphaea 'Emily Grant Hutchings'

The large, cup-like flowers, 15–20cm (6–8in) across, are dark pink with red stamens. The leaves are round, 25–30cm (10–12in) across, bronzy green on top with olive-green undersides.
Approximate spread: 2–2.2m (6–7ft).
Suggested planting depth: 45cm (18in).

Nymphaea 'General Pershing'

The cup-like, scented flowers, which later become flat, are 20–28cm (8–11in) in diameter and have lavender-pink petals surrounding yellow stamens. The round leaves, 23–25cm (9–10in) across, are olive green with purple blotches.
Approximate spread: 1.5–2m (5–6½ft).
Suggested planting depth: 30–45cm (12–18in).

RED
Hardy waterlilies

Nymphaea 'Andreana'

At first cup-like, the peony-style flowers, 13–18cm (5–7in) across, have reddish-orange inner petals and peach-yellow outer petals surrounding deep yellow stamens. The nearly round leaves, 18–20cm (7–8in) in diameter, are green with reddish-brown blotches.
Approximate spread: 1–1.2m (3–4ft).
Suggested planting depth: 30–35cm (12–14in).

Nymphaea 'Arethusa'

The globe-shaped flowers, 13–14cm (5–5½in) across, have dark red petals in the centre with lighter outer petals surrounding orange-red stamens. The round green leaves, 20cm (8in) across, have purple blotches.
Approximate spread: 1–1.2m (3–4ft).
Suggested planting depth: 30–38cm (12–15in).

Nymphaea 'Charles de Meurville'

One of the first waterlilies to flower, the star-shaped flowers, 15–18cm (6–7in) across, have dark, pinkish-red inner petals and pink outer petals around orange stamens. The almost plum-coloured blooms are occasionally streaked with white. The leaves, 25cm (10in) long and 20cm (8in) wide, are dark green with light green veins.
Approximate spread: 1.2–1.5m (4–5ft).
Suggested planting depth: 45–60cm (18–24in).

Nymphaea 'Conqueror'

The star-like flowers, 18–20cm (7–8in) in diameter, have white-flecked, almost crimson petals surrounding long yellow stamens. The round leaves, 25–28cm (10–11in) in diameter, are bronze when young, maturing to deep green.
Approximate spread: 1.5m (5ft).
Suggested planting depth: 30–35cm (12–14in).

Nymphaea 'Escarboucle'

At first cup-shaped, the flowers become star-shaped, about 15–18cm (6–7in) across, with bright vermilion-red petals, the outer ones tipped with white, and deep orange stamens. The brown-tinged young leaves mature to round, green leaves, 25–28cm (10–11in) in diameter. This is one of the best reds for medium and large pools, and it stays open later in the afternoon than most other red varieties.
Approximate spread: 1.2–1.5m (4–5ft).
Suggested planting depth: 30–60cm (1–2ft).

Nymphaea 'Froebelii'

The cup-shaped flowers, which become star-shaped, are 10–13cm (4–5in) across, with burgundy-red petals and orange-red stamens. The young leaves are bronze-red, becoming green, round and 15cm (6in) across. It is ideal for cooler situations and for barrels or small pools.
Approximate spread: 90cm (3ft).
Suggested planting depth: 15–30cm (6–12in).

Nymphaea 'James Brydon'

The cup-shaped flowers, 10–13cm (4–5in) across, have bright rose-red petals and orange-red stamens. Purplish-brown young leaves, blotched with dark purple, mature to round, green leaves 18cm (7in) in diameter. It is ideal for barrels or medium-size pools, both for its flower shape and its free-flowering habit.
Approximate spread: 1–1.2m (3–4ft).
Suggested planting depth: 30–45cm (12–18in).

Nymphaea 'Laydekeri Fulgens'

The cup-shaped flowers of this waterlily, which grow to 13–15cm (5–6in) in diameter, have striking burgundy-red petals surrounding orange-red stamens. The purplish young leaves, which are blotched with dark purple, mature to round, green leaves, reaching 18–20cm (7–8in) in diameter. This is one of the first waterlilies to bloom in spring.
Approximate spread: 1.2–1.5m (4–5ft).
Suggested planting depth: 30–45cm (12–18in).

Nymphaea 'Lucida'

The star-shaped flowers, which are 13–15cm (5–6in) in diameter, have red inner petals and pink-veined, whitish-pink outer petals surrounding yellow stamens. The mature oval leaves grow to 25cm (10in) long and 23cm (9in) wide, with large purple blotches. Suitable for any sized pool, this is a free-flowering form, which has particularly attractive leaves.
Approximate spread: 1.2–1.5m (4–5ft).
Suggested planting depth: 30–45cm (12–18in).

Nymphaea 'Newton'

The star-shaped, red flowers, 15–20cm (6–8in) across, are unusual for a hardy, being carried well above the water when young and floating on the surface on the third day. The narrow petals increase the tropical look and are complemented by deep yellow stamens. The nearly-round leaves are 23cm (9in) across and mid green in colour with purple blotches and brownish red undersides.
Approximate spread: 1.1–1.5m (3½–5ft).
Suggested planting depth: 30cm (12in).

Nymphaea 'Charles de Meurville'

Nymphaea 'Escarboucle'

Nymphaea 'Lucida'

Nymphaea 'Radiant Red'
The star-shaped flowers, 13–15cm (5–6in) in diameter, have long sepals, slightly flecked, deep red petals and orange stamens. The new leaves, which are bronze before turning green, are almost round in shape and reach up to 25cm (10in) in diameter.
Approximate spread: 1–1.2m (3–4ft).
Suggested planting depth: 30–45cm (12–18in).

Nymphaea 'René Gérard'
The star-shaped, rosy-red flowers, 15–23cm (6–9in) across, have flecked, paler red outer petals and yellow stamens. The round, plain green leaves are bronzed when young and grow to 25–28cm (10–11in) across.
Approximate spread: 1.5m (5ft).
Suggested planting depth: 30–45cm (12–18in).

Nymphaea 'Vésuve'
The star-shaped, scented flowers, 17cm (6½in) across, have inward-pointing, red petals, which deepen with age, and orange stamens. The almost circular, green leaves are 23–25cm (9–10in) across. It opens early in the morning and closes late in the afternoon.
Approximate spread: 1.2m (4ft).
Suggested planting depth: 30–45cm (12–18in).

Nymphaea 'William Falconer'
The cup-like flowers, 10–13cm (4–5in) in diameter, have very deep red petals

Nymphaea 'William Falconer'

Nymphaea 'Jennifer Rebecca'

Nymphaea 'René Gérard'

and burgundy-red stamens. The new leaves are purple, maturing to green, and are almost round, 25cm (10in) in diameter. It is ideal for cool areas because it dislikes too much heat and will stop flowering in very hot spells.
Approximate spread: 1m (3ft).
Suggested planting depth: 30–45cm (12–18in).

Tropical waterlilies

Nymphaea 'Evelyn Randig'
The cup-like flowers, which later become star-like, are 18–23cm (7–9in) in diameter and have deep raspberry-pink petals surrounding deep yellow stamens. The beautiful dark green, round leaves, which reach 35–38cm (14–15in) across, have purple blotches covering half of the leaf.
Approximate spread: 1.5–2.2m (5–7ft).
Suggested planting depth: 38–45cm (15–18in).

Nymphaea 'H.C. Haarstick'
A night-blooming waterlily with a pungent scent, the large, flat flowers, 25–3cm (10–12in) across, have red petals surrounding orange-red stamens. The large, round leaves grow to 40cm (16in) and have a reddish-brown tinge and wavy, toothed margins.
Approximate spread: 1.8–3.6m (6–12ft).
Suggested planting depth: 45cm (18in).

Nymphaea 'Jennifer Rebecca'
This is a night-blooming waterlily with dark red flowers shaped like a sunflower, 20–25cm (8–10in) across, and with deep pink stamens. The nearly round leaves, 38cm (15in) across, are reddish brown and sharply dentate, with the edges of the older leaves becoming distinctly wavy.
Approximate spread: 2.2–2.7m (7–9ft).
Suggested planting depth: 45cm (18in).

Nymphaea 'Maroon Beauty'
A night-blooming waterlily, this has huge, flat flowers, measuring 20–25cm (8–10in) across, with deep red petals surrounding reddish-brown and red stamens. The reddish-brown, round leaves are 38cm (15in) in diameter, with toothed leaf margins which become wavy edged as the leaves get older.
Approximate spread: 2.2–2.7m (7–9ft).
Suggested planting depth: 30–45cm (12–18in).

Nymphaea 'Mrs C. W. Ward'
The reddish-pink flowers of this tropical waterlily are star-shaped and 15–20cm (6–8in) in diameter. The flowers have yellow stamens and a most pleasant fragrance. The leaves are egg-shaped and grow to 30–38cm (12–15in) in length. They are green on the top and red underneath with slightly wavy edges. This waterlily requires plenty of space to flourish.
Approximate spread: 2.4m (8ft).
Suggested planting depth: 45cm (18in).

Nymphaea 'Red Flare'
The large, flat, night-blooming flowers, 18–25cm (7–10in) across, have deep red petals and light pink or yellowish stamens. The older leaves, 25–30cm (10–12in) across, become round with a reddish-bronze hue and a few purple blotches, and they have heavily serrated and wavy edges.
Approximate spread: 1.5–1.8m (5–6ft).
Suggested planting depth: 30–45cm (12–18in).

WHITE
Hardy waterlilies

Nymphaea alba
White waterlily
The cup-shaped flowers, 10–13cm (4–5in) in diameter, have rather concave, white petals surrounding yellow stamens. The fresh green leaves, 30cm (12in) across, are red when young and tend to hug the water's surface. This waterlily is not really suitable for small ornamental ponds.
Approximate spread: 1.7m (5½ft).
Suggested planting depth: 60cm (2ft).

Nymphaea 'Gladstoneana'

Nymphaea 'Hermine'

Tropical waterlilies

Nymphaea dentata 'Superba'

This is a night-blooming waterlily which is native to Egypt and also to other parts of Africa. It is sometimes referred to as the "White Nile Lotus". It has large, fragrant white flowers, which grow to 20–25cm (8–10in) in diameter. The flowers are held on hairy flower stalks above the surface of the water. The petals open flat, displaying the attractive yellow stamens. The large leaves are 33cm by 30cm (13 by 12in), dark green above with toothed edges and prominent leaf veins on the underside. This waterlily needs a minimum temperature of 27°C (80°F) to flower well.
Approximate spread: 1.5–1.8m (5–6ft).
Suggested planting depth: 45cm (18in).

Nymphaea 'Marliacea Chromatella'

Nymphaea 'Albatros'

The star-shaped flowers, 15–20cm (6–8in) across, have white petals surrounding yellow stamens.
The round, olive-green leaves, 20–25cm (8–10in) across, have a few purple blotches.
Approximate spread: 1–1.5m (3–5ft).
Suggested planting depth: 30cm (12in).

Nymphaea 'Gladstoneana'

The star-shaped flowers, 13–18cm (5–7in) in diameter, have white petals surrounding yellow stamens. Bronzed young leaves mature to almost round, wavy-edged green leaves, 28–30cm (11–12in) across, with crimped margins along the lobes.
It is very free flowering and best suited to larger pools.
Approximate spread: 1.5–2.4m (5–8ft).
Suggested planting depth: 45–60cm (18–24in).

Nymphaea 'Hermine'

The elegant, star-shaped flowers, 10–15cm (4–6in) across, have long, white petals which are surrounded by golden yellow stamens. The mature leaves are round and green. This magnificent waterlily is moderately vigorous and should be grown in a medium-size pool.
Approximate spread: to 1.8m (6ft).
Suggested planting depth: 15–45cm (6–18in).

Nymphaea 'Marliacea Albida'

The cup-shaped flowers, 13–15cm (5–6in) in diameter, have white petals surrounding yellow stamens. The slightly bronzed young leaves mature to round, green leaves, 23cm (9in) in diameter. This is a good choice for small pools where there is limited space.
Approximate spread: 1–1.2m (3–4ft).
Suggested planting depth: 30–45cm (12–18in).

Nymphaea odorata var. *minor*

The small, star-shaped flowers, which are 8cm (3in) in diameter, have white petals surrounding prominent golden-yellow stamens. The green leaves are almost round, 8–10cm

(3–4in) in diameter, and have dark red undersides. It is a most successful waterlily in tubs or shallow pools, but must have full sun.
Approximate spread: 60cm (2ft).
Suggested planting depth: 23–30cm (9–12in).

Nymphaea tuberosa 'Richardsonii'

The peony-like flowers, 10–23cm (4–9in) in diameter, have white petals surrounding yellow stamens. The round, mid-green leaves are 38cm (15in) across.
Approximate spread: 1.8–2.2m (6–7ft).
Suggested planting depth: 30cm (12in).

Nymphaea 'Virginia'

The fragrant, star-shaped, almost double flowers, 15–18cm (6–7in) in diameter, have creamy, pale yellow petals in the centre and pure white petals on the outside surrounding yellow stamens. The young leaves are green with heavy purple blotching, which becomes restricted to the perimeter of the mature, egg-shaped leaves, which are 25cm (10in) long and 21cm (8½in) wide. This is a classic, free-flowering waterlily.
Approximate spread: 1.5–1.8m (5–6ft).
Suggested planting depth: 30–60cm (1–2ft).

Nymphaea 'Sir Galahad'

This tropical waterlily is vigorous and suitable for a large pool. The star-shaped, white flowers open at night and are held well above the large, waxy leaves, which have crinkled edges. In cold climates, grow under glass in a heated pool.
Approximate spread: to 3m (10ft).
Suggested planting depth: 20–90cm (8–36in).

Nymphaea 'Wood's White Knight'

A full peony-shaped white flower 25–30cm (10–12in) across with yellow stamens and a strong, pungent smell. The nearly-round leaves, 30–38cm (12–15in) across, have wavy and scalloped edges. A superb white for the larger pool.
Approximate spread: 2.4–3m (8–10ft).
Suggested planting depth: 45cm (18in).

YELLOW
Hardy waterlilies

Nymphaea 'Charlene Strawn'

The star-shaped, sweetly-scented flowers, 15–20cm (6–8in) across, have yellow petals surrounding yellow stamens. The nearly round green leaves are 20–23cm (8–9in) in diameter, displaying purple specks when young. This is one of the most fragrant waterlilies.
Approximate spread: 1–1.5m (3–5ft).
Suggested planting depth: 30cm (12in).

Nymphaea 'Marliacea Chromatella'

The cup- to star-shaped flowers, 15cm (6in) in diameter, have broad, incurved, canary-yellow petals and golden stamens. The coppery young leaves with purple streaks mature to attractive purple-mottled, round, green leaves, 15–20cm (6–8in) in diameter.
Approximate spread: 1.2–1.5m (4–5ft).
Suggested planting depth: 30–45cm (12–18in).

Nymphaea 'Sir Galahad'

Nymphaea 'Wood's White Knight'

Nymphaea 'Sioux'

Nymphaea 'Leopardess'

Nymphaea 'Odorata Sulphurea Grandiflora' (syn. *N.* 'Sunrise')

The cup-shaped, later star-shaped, sweet-smelling flowers, which are 15–18cm (6–7in) in diameter, have yellow petals and yellow stamens. The speckled, purple-blotched young leaves mature to broadly ovate green leaves, 25cm (10in) long. The flowers tend to open for only a short time from late morning to early afternoon.
Approximate spread: 1–1.2m (3–4ft).
Suggested planting depth: 30–45cm (12–18in).

Nymphaea 'Pygmaea Helvola' (syn. *N.* × *helvola*)

The cup-shaped, later star-shaped, flowers, which are no more than 5–8cm (2–3in) in diameter, have yellow petals and yellow stamens. The leaves are oval, 13cm (5in) long and 9cm (3½in) wide, heavily mottled and purple-blotched with purple undersides. This delightful small waterlily is a perfect plant for a barrel or sink.
Approximate spread: 60cm (2ft).
Suggested planting depth: 15–23cm (6–9in).

Tropical waterlilies

Nymphaea 'Afterglow'

The flat, sunflower-shaped flowers, 15–25cm (6–10in) in diameter, have yellow petals and golden orange stamens. The leaves are green and nearly round, 28cm (11in) in diameter, with wavy margins and purple undersides. This is a very colourful tropical waterlily.
Approximate spread: 1.8–2.4m (6–8ft).
Suggested planting depth: 30cm (12in).

Nymphaea 'Saint Louis'

The fragrant, star-shaped flowers, 20–28cm (8–11in) across, have lemon-yellow petals and golden-yellow stamens. The purple-blotched young leaves mature to broadly ovate, green leaves, which are occasionally wavy edged and to 50cm (20in) long.
Approximate spread: 2.4–3m (8–10ft).
Suggested planting depth: 38–60cm (15–24in).

CHANGEABLES
Hardy waterlilies

Nymphaea 'Aurora'

The cup-like, later flatter, flowers, 10–12cm (4–4½in) across, have petals that change from yellow-apricot to orange-red then deep burgundy-red on the third day. The leaves, 15–16cm (6–6½in) across, are green with the new leaves blotched purple.
Approximate spread: 1m (3ft).
Suggested planting depth: 25–30cm (10–12in).

Nymphaea 'Indiana'

The cup-like flowers, which when fully open can reach up to 9–10cm (3½–4in) across, have apricot petals, which change to apricot orange, then deep orange-red surrounding glowing orange stamens. The almost round leaves are quite small, eventually reaching 15cm (6in) in diameter. They are initially bronzy green with heavy mottling then become green with purple blotches.
Approximate spread: 75cm (30in).
Suggested planting depth: 23cm (9in).

Nymphaea 'Sioux'

The star-like flowers, 13–15cm (5–6in) across, have long petals, which deepen each day from yellowish-apricot to orange-red then apricot-orange surrounding golden yellow and orange stamens. The round leaves have a dappled purple perimeter when young, maturing to plain green, 20–23cm (8–9in) in diameter.
Approximate spread: 1.2m (4ft).
Suggested planting depth: 23–30cm (9–12in).

BLUE
Tropical waterlilies

Nymphaea 'Blue Beauty'

The fragrant, day-blooming, star-shaped flowers, 20–28cm (8–11in) across, have mauve petals surrounding yellow stamens. The oval, dark green, wavy-margined leaves grow to 35cm (14in) across and have brown speckling on the upper surface. It requires a minimum water temperature of 10°C (50°F).
Approximate spread: 1.2–2.2m (4–7ft).
Suggested planting depth: 38cm (15in).

Nymphaea caerulea

The day-blooming, star-shaped flowers, 15cm (6in) across, have pale blue petals surrounding yellow stamens. The oval, mid-green leaves are 30–40cm (12–16in) long and have purple spotting on the undersides.
Approximate spread: 2.4–3m (8–10ft).
Suggested planting depth: 30–40cm (12–16in).

Nymphaea 'Leopardess'

A day-blooming cultivar with cup-like flowers, 10–13cm (4–5in) across, which are clear blue with purple-tipped petals and yellow stamens. The nearly round, green-blotched purple leaves are green underneath with heavy speckles of purple and 25–30cm (10–12in) across.
Approximate spread: 1.2–1.5m (4–5ft).
Suggested planting depth: 30–45cm (12–18in).

Nymphaea 'Rhonda Kay'

This day-blooming cultivar has star-shaped, violet-blue flowers, 15cm (6in) across, held high above the water, with deep yellow stamens. The leaves are mid-green, slightly longer than they are wide at 28–30cm (11–12in) across.
Approximate spread: 1.8–2.7m (6–9ft).
Suggested planting depth: 45cm (18in).

Nymphaea micrantha

This day-blooming species from the west coast of Africa is free flowering, and can be confused with *N.* × *daubenyana*. The cup-like, later star-shaped, flowers are 2.5–10cm (1–4in) across and pale blue to white with creamy white stamens. The nearly round leaves, 8cm (3in) across, are pale green with reddish undersides. It is the parent species to many wonderful cultivars.
Approximate spread: 60–75cm (2–2½ft).
Suggested planting depth: 30–45cm (12–18in).

Nymphaea 'Blue Beauty'

Nymphaea 'Rhonda Kay'

LOTUS

The genus (*Nelumbo*) contains two species of rhizomatous marginals from Asia, north Australia and eastern North America, where they are found in the shallow margins or muddy banks of pools. They have circular leaves, held horizontally well above the water. Their showy, solitary flowers are borne on long stalks, and develop distinctive "pepper pot" seed-heads. The flowers of the American species, *N. lutea*, approximately 20cm (8in) in diameter, are sulphur-coloured with dark yellow stamens. The Asiatic species, *N. nucifera*, has larger flowers, nearly 30cm (12in) across, with pink or white petals, deep rose on opening, but becoming paler with age. By the end of the third day, the petals are almost creamy white with a rosy-pink blush at the edges.

Lotus need ample sunshine or a high light intensity to ripen the thick roots in the mud. They need a minimum winter temperature of 5°C (41°F), but they will only do their best with a summer temperature of around 20°C (68°F). They can be grown in a large container of rich loam, with at least 30cm (12in) of soil under a covering of 8–15cm (3–6in) of water. Scoop out a depression in the compost for the rootstock, taking care not to damage the crown or growing point. Cover the rhizome with compost, leaving the growing point just sticking out above the surface. Add water and, when there is no danger of frost, stand outside in a hot sunny position. Propagate by dividing the fragile roots, which resent disturbance. In spring, plant the divisions just under the soil surface and just submerge until growth starts.

WHITE

Nelumbo nucifera 'Alba Grandiflora'
The large, white flowers are cup-shaped, 30cm (12in) in diameter, with golden stamens. The leaves grow to 40–58cm (16–23in) across.
Height: 1.2–1.8m (4–6ft); *spread:* indefinite.

Nelumbo nucifera 'Alba Striata'
The fragrant, globe-shaped, white flowers are 25–30cm (10–12cm) across, with the outer petals flushed with pale green and prominent, uneven red margins. The leaves can be as much as 70cm (28in) across.
Height: 1.2–1.5m (4–5ft); *spread:* indefinite.

Nelumbo 'Shiroman' (syn. *N.* var. *alba plena*)
The large, fully double, creamy white flowers are 25cm (10in) in diameter, but have little fragrance. The leaves grow to 62cm (25in) across.
Height: 1–1.5m (3–5ft); *spread:* indefinite.

Nelumbo leaves and seedhead

PINK AND RED

Nelumbo 'Charles Thomas'
The pink flowers are 15–20cm (6–8in) across, deeper at first, then change to a paler lavender-pink. The leaves grow to 35–56cm (14–22in) across.
Height: 60cm–1m (2–3ft); *spread:* indefinite.

Nelumbo 'Maggie Belle Slocum'
The large lavender-pink flowers are 25–30cm (10–12in) in diameter, and the inner petals beautifully rolled. The leaves are 50–62cm (20–25in) across. This lotus is good for tub culture.
Height: 1.2–1.5m (4–5ft); *spread:* indefinite.

Nelumbo nucifera 'Momo Botan'
The peony-like, double, deep rose-pink flowers with yellow bases are 13–15cm (5–6in) in diameter. The leaves have a diameter of 30–38cm (12–15in). The flowers last longer than most other lotuses, also staying open later into the day. This is particularly good for barrels.
Height: to 60cm–1.2m (2–4ft); *spread:* indefinite.

Nelumbo nucifera 'Mrs Perry D. Slocum'
The huge, double flowers are 30cm (12in) across. They open rose pink and change to creamy yellow. The

leaves have a diameter of 45–58cm (18–23in). Because it is a changeable bicolor lotus, there are often different coloured flowers on the plant at the same time.
Height: 1.2–1.5m (4–5ft); *spread:* indefinite.

Nelumbo nucifera 'Pekinensis Rubra'
The slightly fragrant deep rose flowers are 20–30cm (8–12in) in diameter and turn pink as the flower matures. The leaves are 50–60cm (20–24in) across.
Height: 1.2–1.8m (4.6ft); *spread:* indefinite.

Nelumbo nucifera 'Rosea'
The fragrant flowers, which are 20–25cm (8–10in) in diameter, resemble those of a rose and have rose-pink petals and a yellow centre. The leaves are 45–50cm (18–20in) in diameter.
Height: 1.2–1.5m (4–5ft); *spread:* indefinite.

Nelumbo nucifera 'Rosea Plena'
This free-flowering lotus is a double form of *N. nucifera* 'Rosea'. The flowers, 25–33cm (10–13in) across, are a very deep rose pink, and the petals yellow towards the base. The leaves are 45–50cm (18–20in) in diameter.
Height: 1.2–1.5m (4–5ft); *spread:* indefinite.

YELLOW

Nelumbo lutea 'Flavescens'
The yellow flowers are 15–20cm (6–8in) across, with a red spot at the base of each petal. The leaves, like the flowers, have a red spot, and grow to a diameter of 33–43cm (13–17in).
Height: 1–1.5m (3–5ft); *spread:* indefinite.

Nelumbo lutea

MARGINALS

The word "marginal" is used to describe water garden plants that thrive with their roots and the basal part of their stem totally submerged in water or waterlogged soil. Different marginals tolerate different depths of water, and it is important to check that plants which prefer shallow water are not drowned by being too deep, even though in most cases short or seasonal changes in level will be tolerated; deciduous marginals will tolerate more water over their crowns in winter than in summer. Slightly deeper levels of water in the winter will also help to protect certain plants from frost and chilling winds. A good example is *Zantedeschia* (arum lily), which would never survive a severe winter in an ordinary soil outdoors but will be protected under a minimum of 15cm (6in) of water.

Vigorous species of marginals are prevented from invading the centre of the pond when the water becomes too deep for them to survive, which is why it is important to have marginal shelves that are no more than about 23cm (9in) deep when you are making a new pond.

Late spring is a good time to select and purchase marginals, when the new growth is thrusting from the fresh compost. Because so many marginals are vigorous growers it is best to plant them in aquatic containers. The depth of water given for the following marginals is the depth above the crowns and not the actual depth of water. Some containers are as much as 23cm (9in) deep, and the depth of the container should be added to the depth recommended here.

Acorus (Araceae)

The genus contains two perennial species originating in eastern Asia and widespread in the northern hemisphere, where they grow in shallow margins of lakes and ponds. The sword-shaped leaves bear a strong resemblance to those of *Iris*, and they have a distinctive, strong smell when bruised.
Propagation: By dividing the rhizomes into pieces, each containing two or three buds.
Hardiness: Hardy to half hardy.

Acorus calamus

Sweet flag, myrtle flag
This hardy, widespread plant is a vigorous species, ideal for a wildlife pool. Like many vigorous, temperate marginals, it is a good cover plant for waterfowl but does not have the piercing root tips and almost uncontrollable spreading habit of *Typha* (reedmace). The long, glossy sword-shaped leaves have a distinct midrib, and part of the leaf edge is noticeably crinkled. The flower is inconspicuous and unusual, resembling a small brown horn, which emerges at an angle just below the tip of a leaf.
Cultivation: Grow in full sun in water to 23cm (9in) deep.
Height: 60cm–1m (2–3ft); *spread:* indefinite.

Acorus calamus 'Argenteostriatus'

This is a much superior form for pools, where the cream-striped leaves make a striking impact in the margins. The variegation is maintained throughout summer, unlike the similar *Iris pseudacorus* 'Variegata' (variegated flag iris), which goes green by midsummer. It is slightly slower growing than *A. calamus*.
Cultivation: Grow in full sun in water to 23cm (9in) deep.
Height: 60cm–1m (2–3ft); *spread:* 60cm (2ft).

Acorus gramineus

Japanese rush
This is a much smaller plant than *A. calamus*, with a rather fan-like habit and glossy, sedge-like leaves that are semi-evergreen. It is slightly vulnerable in severe winters if the roots are not covered with water about 5–8cm (2–3in) deep. It will tolerate a very wide range of soil conditions, from being submerged in shallow water to being grown as a pot plant. There are some excellent cultivars, including 'Variegatus' (variegated Japanese rush), with striped creamy leaves, and 'Hakuro-nishiki', with pale green variegated leaves.
Cultivation: Grow in full sun in pond margins.
Height: 8–35cm (3–14in); *spread:* 10–15cm (4–6in).

Alisma (Alismataceae)

The nine species of aquatics in the genus are found across the world, but mainly in the northern hemisphere, where they grow in the muddy edges of marshes and lakes. The seeds,

Acorus calamus

which are valuable food for wildlife, are the main method of propagation. They are produced in abundance and are capable of floating some distance. Unlike most aquatic seeds, they remain viable for up to a year.
Propagation: By seed or by division.
Hardiness: Hardy.

Alisma plantago-aquatica

Water plantain
This deciduous perennial has rosettes of oval, grey to grey-green, semi-upright, ribbed leaves, which have long leaf stalks that emerge well above the water. The tiny pinky-white

Alisma plantago-aquatica

flowers have three petals and are arranged in whorls on a pyramidal spike in midsummer.
Cultivation: Grow in a sunny position in water to 15cm (6in) deep.
Height: 75cm (30in); *spread:* 45cm (18in).

Butomus (Butomaceae)

A genus containing a single species of marginal perennial, which is found widely distributed in Europe, western Asia and north Africa and which has naturalized along the St Lawrence river near Montreal in North America.
Propagation: By removing the bulbils, which grow along the roots, and potting these individually in small pots of aquatic compost, or by dividing the rootstock in mid-spring.
Hardiness: Hardy.

Butomus umbellatus

Flowering rush, flowering gladiolus
Often found growing singly in the wild among a clump of reedmaces, it has long, dark green, pointed, narrow twisted leaves, with sheathed, triangular bases. The elegant flowers are borne above the leaves in a rounded pink flower-head.
Cultivation: Grow in rich mud or shallow water no deeper than 8–15cm (3–6in).
Height: 1m (3ft); *spread:* 45cm (18in).

Butomus umbellatus

Calla (Araceae)

A genus containing one species of perennial marginal from central and northern Europe, northern Asia and North America, where it is found in swamps, bogs and wet woods. In mild winters it is semi-evergreen.
Propagation: By dividing the surface root in spring, making sure that each piece contains a bud.
Hardiness: Hardy.

Calla palustris
Bog arum
The bog arum has conspicuous, long, creeping surface roots and round to heart-shaped, glossy, mid-green leaves, which are firm and leathery. The flowers, which appear in spring, resemble small, flattened arum lilies, and they are followed by clusters of red or orange berries.
Cultivation: Grow in full sun in water no deeper than 5cm (2in).
Height: 25cm (10in); *spread:* indefinite in the right conditions, but usually about 30cm (12in).

Caltha (Ranunculaceae)

This is a widespread and common genus containing ten species of temperate marginals, which are extremely popular in both decorative and wildlife ponds.
Propagation: By seed (apart from the double forms) or by division immediately after flowering.
Hardiness: Hardy to frost hardy.

Caltha palustris
Marsh marigold, kingcup
Indispensable for the pond margins, the native hardy marsh marigold needs little introduction. It has long-stalked lower leaves and stalkless upper leaves. The leaves are nearly round, heart-shaped at the base, and have toothed margins. The beautiful, waxy, yellow, buttercup-like flowers can appear as early as late winter in a mild season but are generally at their peak in mid-spring, when they brighten the spring garden, particularly when they are planted near the blue flowers of *Muscari* (grape hyacinth). They look best in groups in a sunny or partly shaded position at the very edge of the water, and they tolerate waterlogged or even slightly submerged conditions in winter and a degree of drying out in the summer. The white marsh marigold, *C. palustris* var. *alba*, differs from the common marsh marigold in having white flowers with yellow centres and a slightly more compact habit. The

double form, *C. palustris* 'Flore Pleno', covers its foliage with a mass of double yellow flowers, often producing a second flush in the summer.
Cultivation: Grow in sun or partial shade in water no deeper than 10–15cm (4–6in).
Height: 15–30cm (6–12in); *spread:* 45cm (18in).

Caltha palustris var. *palustris* (syn. *C. laeta*, *C. polypetala*)
Giant marsh marigold
This massive plant is suitable only for growing by the side of large ponds, where it can send its large yellow flowers on long stems as high as 1m (3ft). The dark green leaves are as much as 25–30cm (10–12in) across, forming strong hummocks of foliage.
Cultivation: Grow in sun in water to 10–13cm (4–5in) deep.
Height: 1m (3ft); *spread:* 75cm (30in).

Canna (Cannaceae)
Indian shot plant
The genus contains nine species that are native to tropical and subtropical America and that are used mainly as decorative terrestrial plants, but there is one species suitable for immersing in pools for the summer where it makes a showy specimen plant.
Propagation: By seed or by division of the rhizomes in spring so that each section has a prominent "eye".
Hardiness: Half hardy to frost tender.

Canna glauca
This tender species has long, slender stems with long, greyish, pointed leaves with whitish margins to 45cm (18in) long. Yellow flower spikes are produced intermittently throughout the summer. Several excellent

Caltha palustris

Carex riparia

Carex pendula

cultivars have been produced at Longwood Gardens in Pennsylvania, including *C.* 'Endeavour' (bright red), *C.* 'Erebus' (bright pink) and *C.* 'Taney' (bright orange).
Cultivation: Grow in a sunny position in containers of rich soil and submerged in water no deeper than 30cm (12in).
Height: 1.2–1.8m (4–6ft); *spread:* 50cm (20in).

Carex (Cyperaceae)
Sedge
This is a large genus, containing about 1,000 species of mainly temperate marsh plants, found throughout the world. They prefer slightly acid conditions, but some species are able to thrive in shallow water. All have grasslike, narrow leaves and triangular flower stalks bearing flowers in brownish spikes. See also the section on ornamental grasses.
Propagation: By division of the strong rhizomes.
Hardiness: Hardy to frost tender (unless otherwise stated).

Carex elata 'Aurea' (syn. *C. stricta* 'Aurea', *C. stricta* 'Bowles' Golden')
Bowles' golden sedge
This plant is particularly valuable in bringing a touch of yellow to the water's edge. It grows in dense tufts of bright grassy leaves. The flowers appear in early spring before the leaves turn bright yellow.
Cultivation: Grow in full sun or partial shade submerged in shallow water to 15cm (6in) deep or in an ordinary soil, kept constantly moist.
Height: 38cm (15in); *spread:* 45cm (18in).

Carex pendula
Pendulous sedge, drooping sedge
Ample space by the waterside and partial shade is required for the long spikes of pendulous flowers, which are held on stems 1m (3ft) long above the thick tufts of grassy leaves.
Cultivation: Grow in water no deeper than 2.5–5cm (1–2in).
Height: 60cm–1m (2–3ft); *spread:* 1.5m (5ft).

Carex pseudocyperus
Hardy to frost hardy, this is one of the more graceful of the sedges. It has bright green, grassy leaves, and the flowers form drooping dark green spikelets in the summer.
Cultivation: Grow in partial shade.
Height and spread: 60cm–1m (2–3ft).

Carex riparia
Great pond sedge
A coarse, tough plant, this is suitable only for the margins of a large wildlife pool. It has acutely triangular stems and leaf blades with a deep midrib. It often forms dense masses of leaves supporting a further cluster of foliage and flowers above.
Cultivation: Grow in sun or shade in water to 10–15cm (4–6in) deep.
Height: 1.5m (5ft); *spread:* 1–1.2m (3–4ft).

Colocasia (Araceae)
Taro
The genus of seven tropical species from Asia contains some species that thrive in shallow water and make bold architectural plants. In temperate areas they should be grown in reliably frost-free conservatories.
Propagation: By division of the rootstock in spring.
Hardiness: Frost tender.

Colocasia esculenta (syn. *C. antiquorum*)

Green taro

This striking plant forms an erect, tuberous rootstock, which bears long-stalked, arrow- to heart-shaped leaves that resemble elephants' ears. The leaf stalks are 8–25cm (3–10in) in length and the leaf blade grows up to 1m (3ft) long. The leaves vary in colour, often having prominent veins, which add to the ornamental value. The flowers, which are rather insignificant spathes, are borne during the summer. *C. esculenta* 'Fontanesii' has heart-shaped leaves with dark green veining and margins and violet leaf stalks.
Cultivation: Grow in partial shade to protect the leaves from sun scorch.
Height: 1.5m (5ft); *spread:* 60cm (2ft).

Colocasia esculenta

Cyperus involucratus

Equisetum hyemale

Cotula (Asteraceae)

Brass buttons

A cosmopolitan genus of about 75 mainly terrestrial species, which are found mostly in the southern hemisphere. One species can be considered as a true aquatic.
Propagation: By seed.
Hardiness: Frost hardy to half hardy.

Cotula coronopifolia

Bachelor's buttons, golden buttons

The various common names give a clue to the flower shape of this bright little marginal. It is an annual or short-lived, half-hardy perennial with several creeping succulent stems and strongly

scented, toothed leaves. The plant is covered with masses of disc-shaped yellow flowers about 1cm (½in) in diameter. It tends to die down in the winter but regenerates easily in the spring from the masses of self-sown seed produced throughout the year.
Cultivation: Grow in full sun in shallow water 8–10cm (3–4in) deep.
Height: 15–30cm (6–12in); *spread:* to 30cm (12in).

Cyperus (Cyperaceae)

This large genus contains about 600 predominantly tropical species with a very wide distribution but only a few

temperate species. They are often referred to as umbrella sedges, and some are impressive in stature and can be grown as specimen clumps in conservatories or outdoor ponds.
Propagation: By seed or by division in the spring.
Hardiness: Hardy to frost tender.

Cyperus involucratus (syn. *C. alternifolius*)

Umbrella plant

This distinctive, tender perennial, which originates from Africa, can be grown as a houseplant as long as it is kept in a saucer of water, and is often, in fact, sold as a houseplant. In warm sheltered pools in subtropical gardens it makes an elegant marginal, the erect stems topped with several dark green radiating leaves. In the summer, tiny yellow flowers form clusters, 13cm (5in) across, at the top of the stems in the leaf axils, and turn brown after pollination.
Cultivation: Full sun or partial shade. Requires a minimum temperature of 5–10°C (41–50°F).
Height and spread: 60–75cm (24–30in).

Cyperus longus

Sweet galingale

The sweet galingale is one of the few hardy members of the genus and is a particularly attractive colonizer of muddy banks. It can spread very quickly so should be kept restricted to containers in small ponds. The almost triangular stems bear interesting, bright green, stiffly ribbed leaves that radiate from the top of the stem like the ribs of an umbrella. The brown flowers are rather inconspicuous spikelets interspersed among the leaves. It is an excellent plant for the wildlife

pool, particularly in late summer and autumn when the arching brown flowers come into their own.
Cultivation: Grow in full sun or partial shade.
Height: 60cm–1.2m (2–4ft); *spread:* 1m (3ft) or more.

Cyperus papyrus

Egyptian paper reed, giant papyrus

When grown in a sheltered, tropical situation or in a conservatory in temperate areas, this will make a tall, elegant specimen. It produces a thick rootstock with long, triangular, pithy stems, bearing mop-head tufts of fine long pendulous leaves and spikelets of brown flowers.
Cultivation: Grow in full sun and protect from wind.
Height: 3.6–4.5m (12–15ft); *spread:* 60cm–1.2m (2–4ft).

Equisetum (Equisetaceae)

Horsetail

The genus contains about 25 species from wet places in most regions of the world except Australia and New Zealand. Do not introduce any of the species into marginal beds where there is no restriction to their spreading.
Propagation: By division from spring to autumn.
Hardiness: Hardy.

Equisetum hyemale

Scouring rush, rough horsetail

This is an evergreen species. The hollow, leafless stems are ridged. A brownish pollen cone is produced at the tip of the spikes.
Cultivation: Grow in moist soil or covered with up to 20cm (8in) of water.
Height: 1.2m (4ft); *spread:* indefinite.

Cotula coronopifolia

Eriophorum angustifolium

Glyceria maxima var. *variegata*

Equisetum scirpoides
A smaller species with fine, multi-branched, soft stems, which can be impressive in a half barrel or stone trough of water. The semi-prostrate, light green stems will spread indefinitely unless grown in a container.
Cultivation: Grow in full sun or partial shade in shallow water no deeper than 5cm (2in).
Height: 15cm (6in); *spread:* indefinite.

Eriophorum (Cyperaceae)
Cotton grass
A genus of 20 species found in bogs, marshes and shallow water margins of lakes and pools in most northern temperate regions. It spreads rapidly, particularly in acid conditions.
Propagation: By breaking off pieces from the clumps of spreading rootstocks.
Hardiness: Hardy.

Eriophorum angustifolium
Common cotton grass
Cotton grass is a widespread plant found in bogs, grown for the conspicuous white tassels of cotton-like flowers. Out of flower it is a rather dull plant, with short, leafy and angled stems, which will spread to form large clumps.

Houttuynia cordata 'Chameleon'

Cultivation: Grow in full sun and where it will not be covered by more than 5cm (2in) of water for any length of time.
Height: 30cm (12in); *spread:* indefinite.

Glyceria (Poaceae)
Manna grass, sweet grass
A widespread genus of 16 temperate species of aquatic grasses that quickly colonize the edges of streams and ponds. All species are extremely rapid spreaders and need to be kept in check.
Propagation: By dividing the creeping rootstocks.
Hardiness: Hardy to frost tender.

Glyceria maxima var. variegata (syn. G. spectabilis 'Variegata')
This highly ornamental, hardy aquatic grass deserves a place in the ornamental pond provided it is planted in an aquatic container. It has very striking leaves, which are striped cream, white and green, and in spring the young leaves are flushed with pink. The flowers form greenish spikelets in summer. It is very easy to grow.
Cultivation: Grow in full sun (for the best leaf colours) in water to 15cm (6in) deep.
Height: 60cm (2ft); *spread:* indefinite.

Houttuynia (Saururiaceae)
The genus contains a single species of temperate aquatic plant from eastern Asia. It flourishes in wet soil or the shallow margins of ponds and streams, producing extensive mats of shallow rhizomes.
Propagation: By dividing rhizomes in spring.
Hardiness: Borderline hardy.

Houttuynia cordata
This useful clump-forming, hardy perennial has spreading roots and erect, leafy red stems. The bluish-green, leathery, pointed leaves give off a pungent smell when crushed. In spring spikes of rather insignificant flowers surrounded by white bracts are produced. It is on the borderline of hardiness and requires the protection of a thick, leafy mulch in autumn. *H. cordata* can be invasive and should be grown in a container in a small pool.
Cultivation: Grow in a partially shaded position in water no deeper than 2.5–5cm (1–2in).
Height: 45–50cm (18–20in); *spread:* indefinite.

Houttuynia cordata 'Chameleon' (syn. H. c. 'Tricolor')
The leaves of this colourful cultivar are splashed with crimson, green and cream.
Cultivation: Grow in full sun (for the complete colour range) in water no deeper than 2.5–5cm (1–2in).
Height: 45–50cm (18–20in); *spread:* indefinite.

Iris (Iridaceae)
This is a large, widely distributed genus containing about 300 mainly temperate, moisture-loving species, and it is one of the most important groups in the water garden. All species have a wide tolerance of degrees of moisture, but the three described here are the most suitable for growing with their roots submerged in water. Some other species are described in the section on moisture-loving plants.
Propagation: By division of the rootstock in spring.
Hardiness: Hardy to frost tender. (Those described here are hardy.)

Iris laevigata
This species produces clumps of sword-shaped, soft green leaves. The sparsely branched stems bear between two and four broad-petalled, beardless, blue flowers in early summer. When it is not in flower, *I. laevigata* can be confused with *I. ensata* (syn. *I. kaempferi*), the Japanese iris, which has large, showy flowers but is not a true marginal, dying if the roots remain underwater in winter. The leaves of *I. laevigata* lack a midrib, while those of *I. ensata* have a distinct midrib. Of the many excellent cultivars of *I. laevigata*, one of the most impressive is 'Variegata', which has pale, lavender-blue flowers and lovely cream-and-white-striped leaves. 'Atropurpurea' has single, purple flowers; 'Richard Greany' has sky-blue single flowers; 'Snowdrift' has beautiful white single flowers; and 'Weymouth Blue' has blue single flowers.
Cultivation: Grow in water no deeper than 8–10cm (3–4in).
Height: 60cm–1m (2–3ft); *spread:* indefinite.

Iris pseudacorus
Flag iris
This vigorous perennial is often seen in sunny or shaded positions in ditches and along the margins of natural ponds and lakes. The strong, stiff, bluish-green, sword-shaped

Iris laevigata 'Snowdrift'

Juncus ensifolius

leaves, to 1m (3ft) long, emerge from a thick rhizome, which will spread for some distance, binding the soil surface. The tall, branched flower stems bear as many as ten beardless flowers on each stem. Each flower is yellow, with brownish veins and a deeper orange spot in the throat. It is ideal for the margins of a wildlife pool.
Cultivation: Grow in 15–30cm (6–12in) of water.
Height: 1–1.8m (3–6ft); *spread:* indefinite.

Iris pseudacorus var. bastardii
This form is not quite as vigorous as *I. pseudacorus* but has lovely, creamy yellow flowers, much lighter in colour.
Cultivation: Grow in 15–30cm (6–12in) of water.
Height: 1–1.8m (3–6ft); *spread:* indefinite.

Iris pseudacorus 'Variegata'
This is an excellent variegated form, which is suitable for small pools if it is grown in a container. The leaves have a striking, creamy-striped variegation, which appears in spring and gradually fades as the summer advances.
Cultivation: Grow in 15–30cm (6–12in) of water.
Height: 1–1.8m (3–6ft); *spread:* indefinite.

Iris versicolor
Blue flag
This free-flowering species is similar in vigour to *I. laevigata* and can spread extensively. The flowers are violet blue with yellow patches at the petal bases. The sword-shaped leaves are to 60cm (2ft) long.
Cultivation: Grow in permanently wet soil or with no more than 10cm (4in) of water above the roots.
Height: 60cm (2ft); *spread:* indefinite.

Juncus (Juncaceae)
Bog rush
This is a large cosmopolitan genus, containing more than 220 species, which are more prevalent in the northern hemisphere, where they occur mainly in marshes and bogs. Commonly referred to as rushes, their appearance is more similar to that of grasses, and they often have flattened leaves sheathed at the base.
Propagation: By dividing the grassy clumps in spring.
Hardiness: Hardy.

Juncus effusus
Common rush, soft rush
Forming ornamental tufts or clumps of green spikes, this species is used in large wildlife pools. It produces brown flower spikes.
Cultivation: Grow in full sun or partial shade with 8–13cm (3–5in) of water over the roots.
Height: 1m (3ft); *spread:* indefinite.

Juncus effusus f. spiralis
Corkscrew rush
This is a hardy form with dark green, needlelike leaves that are contorted or corkscrew-like. They create a point of interest in the shallows of a small pond.
Cultivation: Grow in full sun with no more than 8–13cm (3–5in) of water over the crown.
Height: 45cm (18in); *spread:* 30–40cm (12–16in).

Juncus ensifolius
This small member of the rush family is a charming hardy marginal for the side of a small pool and is particularly good for the side of a stream. It prefers very damp, mostly wet banks, where it looks best in groups. It produces neat tufts of grassy foliage and attractive round brown flower spikes.
Cultivation: Grow in full sun in water no deeper than 5cm (2in).
Height: 30cm (12in); *spread:* indefinite.

Lysichiton (Araceae)
Skunk cabbage
The genus contains two temperate species of perennial bog plants from North America, Siberia and Japan. The unfortunate common name refers to the scent of the flowers.
Propagation: The thick roots grow deeply into a moist soil and become difficult to divide; propagation is best by seed.
Hardiness: Hardy.

Lysichiton americanus
Yellow skunk cabbage
This impressive plant provides an early spring display of yellow, aroid-like flowers, which are followed by huge, almost stalkless, paddle-like leaves capable of growing to almost 1.2m (4ft) high and spreading to 90cm (3ft).
Cultivation: Grow in full sun in no more than 2.5cm (1in) of water.
Height: 1.2m (4ft); *spread:* 1m (3ft).

Lysichiton camschatcensis
White skunk cabbage
This species, which has white flowers, is less vigorous than the more common *L. americanus* and is therefore more suitable for the margins of a small pond. The leaves are mottled and paddle-shaped, growing semi-upright from ground level with little or no leaf stalk.
Cultivation: Grow in full sun. It is on the borderline of tolerance to having shallow water over the roots, but provided there is a deep saturated soil it will not mind short periods of being submerged by shallow water.
Height and spread: 60–75cm (24–30in).

Iris versicolor

Iris laevigata 'Atropurpurea'

Mentha (Lamiaceae)

This is a genus of 25 species of temperate, aromatic plants, which prefer moist conditions and spread rapidly by underground rhizomes. The genus includes one species that will thrive in aquatic conditions and is now widely available as a marginal.
Propagation: By dividing the long, thin roots in spring and summer.
Hardiness: Hardy.

Mentha aquatica

Water mint
Common in ditches and alongside running water, water mint has lilac-coloured flowers, produced in terminal whorls above hairy, egg-shaped leaves with serrated margins.
Cultivation: Grow in full sun or partial shade. It can survive in a wide range of water depths but does best in water no deeper than 15cm (6in).
Height: 1m (3ft); *spread:* 1m (3ft) or more.

Menyanthes
(Menyanthaceae)

Bog bean, marsh trefoil, buck bean
The single species in the genus is a temperate aquatic, distributed throughout North America, northern Asia, Europe and northwestern India. It is common in shallow pools and

acid bogs, where its thick, spongy, creeping rootstocks quickly colonize the edges.
Propagation: By dividing the extensive roots in spring.
Hardiness: Hardy.

Menyanthes trifoliata

This excellent hardy perennial will quickly colonize the shallow waters at the margins of a large, sunny pool, as its thick, spongy rootstock spreads just underneath the surface of the water. The attractive foliage is clover-like, shiny, olive-green leaves, made up of three leaflets, with a long leaf stalk that clasps the spreading roots with a broad sheath. The flowers are particularly appealing. Dense spikes of dainty, frilled, white to purplish flowers emerge from pink buds and are held above the surface of the water. In a large, wildlife pool it provides excellent cover for submerged creatures in the shallow margins and can spread to form clumps of 1m (3ft) across or more in one year.
Cultivation: Grow in sun in water about 5cm (2in) deep. Containerize in a small pool and cut back hard any escaping roots each spring.
Height: 25–40cm (10–16in); *spread:* indefinite.

Mentha aquatica

Menyanthes trifoliata

Mimulus
(Scrophulariaceae)

Musk, monkey flower
The genus contains about 150 temperate and subtropical species, native to North America, South Africa and Asia but not occurring naturally in Europe. Most of the species appreciate moisture-rich conditions, and a few make striking marginal plants.
Propagation: By seed.
Hardiness: Hardy to frost tender.

Mimulus guttatus
(syn. *M. langsdorffii*)

Monkey musk, common monkey flower
This is a hardy species which originates from western North America. It grows submerged in water during the winter and produces aerial shoots in summer. It grows from robust stems, which have oval, toothed leaves and masses of yellow flowers. The flowers are marked with a pair of reddish-brown, hairy ridges.
Cultivation: Grow in full sun.
Height: 35–100cm (14–40in); *spread:* 50–120cm (20–48in).

Mimulus luteus

Yellow monkey flower
This is a vigorous, hardy species, which has prostrate, smooth, hollow stems. These stems root at the nodes and carry several bright yellow flowers with deep-red or purple spots.
Cultivation: Grow in full sun or light dappled shade.
Height: 10–30cm (4–12in); *spread:* 60cm (2ft).

Mimulus ringens

Allegheny monkey flower, lavender musk
This hardy species has branching square stems with dark green, narrowly oblong leaves. The blue to bluish-violet, snapdragon-like flowers are about 2.5cm (1in) long with a very narrow throat.
Cultivation: Grow in full sun in moist soil or in shallow water no deeper than 8–13cm (3–5in).
Height: 45cm (18in); *spread:* 30cm (12in).

Myosotis (Boraginaceae)

Forget-me-not
This genus of 50 temperate species, which are most commonly found in Europe and Australia and naturalized in North America, includes a few attractive aquatic forms that are indispensable to the water gardener.
Propagation: By stem cuttings from the young growth in spring or by division in spring or early summer.
Hardiness: Hardy.

Myosotis scorpioides

Water forget-me-not
This attractive hardy marginal has a slightly looser and more delicate habit of growth than most of the more rampant marginals. It bears the most delightful light blue flowers with yellow centres in midsummer. The angular stems are almost upright, becoming fully erect at the tips. The loose habit of growth combined with the delicacy of the small leaves and flower colourings makes this one of the

Mimulus guttatus

Orontium aquaticum

Ranunculus lingua

most sought-after marginals for ponds of all sizes. 'Mermaid' is an improved cultivar that is more free-flowering than the species.
Cultivation: Grow in full sun or light dappled shade in no more than 8cm (3in) of water.
Height: 23–30cm (9–12in); *spread:* 30cm (12in).

Orontium (Araceae)
Golden club
The genus contains a single species from temperate areas of eastern North America, where it grows in bogs or shallow water.
Propagation: By sowing seed as soon as it is ripe in midsummer.
Hardiness: Hardy.

Orontium aquaticum
This hardy species produces large, bluish-green, velvety, lance-shaped leaves with a silvery sheen on the undersides. The shades of the leaves are best appreciated when the plant is grown as a specimen. The white-stalked, pencil-shaped flowers that emerge from the water, tipped with yellow, resemble small golden pokers.
Cultivation: Grow in full sun in water between 38–45cm (15–18in) deep. In water deeper than 30cm (12in) the leaves float on the surface.
Height: 45cm (18in); *spread:* 75cm (30in).

Peltandra (Araceae)
Arrow arum
The genus contains two species from temperate North America, closely related to the arums. They are suitable

for muddy margins or shallow water, scrambling over the surface, with the long rhizomes rooting at the nodes.
Propagation: By dividing sections of the rhizomes in spring so that each section contains a bud.
Hardiness: Hardy.

Peltandra sagittifolia (syn. *P. alba*)
White arrow arum
The hardy species has strong, bright green, arrow-shaped and veined leaves growing from a short rhizome. The arum-like flowers are white, about 8–10cm (3–4in) long, and are followed by fleshy red berries in late summer.
Cultivation: Grow in full sun in water no deeper than 10–15cm (4–6in).
Height: 45cm (18in); *spread:* 60cm (2ft).

Peltandra undulata (syn. *P. virginica*)
Green arrow arum
This species is distinguished from *P. sagittifolia* by its narrower and greener flower spathe, which produces red rather than green berries. The firm leaves are narrowly arrow shaped.
Cultivation: Grow in full sun in water no deeper than 10–15cm (4–6in).
Height: 75cm (30in); *spread:* 60cm (2ft).

Persicaria (Polygonaceae)
The large genus contains about 80 species, some of which were previously classified as *Bistorta, Polygonum* and *Tovara*. The species are found in tropical and temperate areas throughout the world, and many are excellent moisture-loving plants, with one species suitable for marginal planting.
Propagation: By stem cuttings in midsummer.
Hardiness: Hardy to frost hardy.

Persicaria amphibia
Amphibious bistort, willow grass
A hardy, stem-rooting perennial, this is useful for pools with a

Peltandra undulata

fluctuating water level. The lance-shaped leaves clasp the stem with long petioles that emerge from a papery sheath. The flowers form neat pink spikes.
Cultivation: Grow in full sun in water 30cm–1m (1–3ft) deep.
Height: 30–60cm (1–2ft); *spread:* indefinite.

Pontederia (Pontederiaceae)
This genus of shallow-water plants from temperate and subtropical areas in North and South America contains just five species. They are useful plants for both formal and informal water gardens, having a strong shape and blue flower in late summer.
Propagation: By division in late spring.
Hardiness: Hardy to frost hardy.

Pontederia cordata
Pickerel weed
This hardy, perennial marginal is undoubtedly one of the most decorative blue-flowered plants available from aquatic suppliers. It is a robust, tidy plant. The thick, creeping rootstock supports shiny, erect, heart-shaped leaves, which are olive green with exquisite swirled markings. A delightful soft blue flower spike appears from a leaf bract at the top of the stem.
Cultivation: Grow with up to 13cm (5in) of water above its crown. Plant in full sun so that it shows off its full flowering potential.
Height: 45–60cm (18–24in); *spread:* 75cm (30in).

Ranunculus (Ranunculaceae)
There are about 400 species of temperate and tropical moisture-loving and aquatic plants in this large, cosmopolitan genus. Of these, almost 40 grow in water.
Propagation: By division in spring and summer.
Hardiness: Hardy.

Ranunculus flammula
Lesser spearwort
This hardy perennial member of the buttercup family is suitable for a small pool, unlike many of its relatives, which can be rank growers. Although this plant is most at home in the shallows of a wildlife pool, it can be containerized easily. It makes a good low-growing spread of yellow flowers over a long season in a smaller pond, producing

semi-prostrate, reddish stems and dark green, lance-shaped leaves, 1–2.5cm (½–1in) long. The shallowly cup-shaped, bright yellow flowers, 2cm (¾in) in diameter, are borne in clusters in early summer.
Cultivation: Grow in full sun or partial shade.
Height: 60cm (2ft); *spread:* 1m (3ft).

Ranunculus lingua
Greater spearwort
This is a hardy, vigorous plant, with hollow, reddish stems. The long-stalked, heart-shaped leaves grow on the non-flowering shoots, and narrower, longer leaves with short stalks grow on the flowering shoots. The large yellow flowers are 2.5–5cm (1–2in) across. Its rather sappy growth means that it is easily blown over in exposed situations.
Cultivation: Grow in full sun in water up to 23cm (9in) deep.
Height: 1.5m (5ft); *spread:* 1.8m (6ft).

Sagittaria (Alismataceae)
A cosmopolitan genus, there are 20 species of aquatics found in a wide variety of habitats, but mainly in shallow water, on muddy shores and in marshes. They are often referred to as duck potatoes because the over-wintering tubers on the ends of their roots are often eaten by wildfowl. In deep water these plants produce only submerged, ribbon-like leaves, but when they are grown in the pond margins they produce their more characteristic arrow-shaped leaves.
Propagation: By division in spring.
Hardiness: Hardy to frost tender.

Sagittaria latifolia

Schoenoplectus lacustris subsp.
tabernaemontani 'Zebrinus'

Scrophularia auriculata 'Variegata'

Cultivation: Grow in full sun
(to encourage the colour of the
stems) in water to 15cm (6in) deep.
Cut out any all-green stems.
Height: 1.2–1.5m (4–5ft); *spread:*
indefinite.

Schoenoplectus lacustris subsp. *tabernaemontani* 'Zebrinus'
Zebra rush
This variegated bulrush is very
effective in groups around the edge
of a large pond. This cultivar has
horizontal cream stripes on the stems,
which resemble porcupine quills. The
inconspicuous flowers appear at the
tips of the long leafless stems in the
form of a brown spikelet.
Cultivation: Grow in full sun (to
maintain the cream banding) in water
8–10cm (3–4in) deep. Cut out any
all-green stems.
Height: 1–1.2m (3–4ft); *spread:*
indefinite.

Sagittaria latifolia
Duck potato, wapato
This is a hardy plant, which will
tolerate a wide range of water depths.
In shallow water it grows arrow-
shaped leaves 10–30cm (4–12in) long
and bears whorls of three-petalled
white flowers in summer. Short
branching tubers are produced on
the tips of the roots.
Cultivation: Grow in full sun in water
to 30cm (12in) deep.
Height: 45–90cm (18–36in); *spread:*
1m (3ft).

Sagittaria sagittifolia (syn. *S. japonica*)
Arrowhead
This hardy species is not quite as
vigorous as *S. latifolia*. The arrow-
shaped leaves, which grow to
20–25cm (8–10in), have long, acute
basal lobes. The white flowers are
borne on three angled stems in
whorls of three with a purple blotch
at the base of each petal.
Cultivation: Grow in full sun in water
no deeper than 15cm (6in).
Height: 1m (3ft); *spread:* indefinite.

Sagittaria sagittifolia 'Flore Pleno'
This handsome, hardy, double form
has round, double white flowers,
about 2.5cm (1in) in diameter,
arranged around a spike.
Cultivation: Grow in full sun in
water no deeper than 5cm (2in)
because flowering will be restricted
in deeper water.
Height: 1m (3ft); *spread:* indefinite.

Saururus (Saururaceae)
Lizard's tail
The genus contains two shallow-
water, clump-forming species from
North America and east Asia.
The common name refers to the
distinctive pendulous flower spikes.
Propagation: By division in spring.
Hardiness: Hardy.

Saururus cernuus
American swamp lily
This is a rampant plant in shallow
water. It has heart-shaped, bright
green leaves and tiny, fragrant, white
flowers held in a nodding, semi-
pendulous spike, 10–15cm (4–6in)
long in late summer.
Cultivation: Grow in water 10cm
(4in) deep. It prefers full sun but
will tolerate light shade.
Height: 30–60cm (1–2ft); *spread:*
30cm (1ft).

Schoenoplectus (Cyperaceae)
Bulrush
The 80 species in the genus are widely
distributed in temperate and tropical
areas, found in marshes and shallow
water. Bulrushes have very long stems,
which grow from a rampant stolon,
and for this reason they need to be
kept in a container in a small pool.
They look best grown as a group at
the side of a large wildlife pool.
Propagation: By division of the
extensive rootstock during spring and
summer.
Hardiness: Hardy.

Schoenoplectus lacustris subsp. *tabernaemontani* 'Albescens'
The erect, cylindrical stems have
attractive cream banding which runs
the length of the stem, making a bold
display when they are seen against a
dark background. The flowers are
insignificant brown spikelets held
on the tips of the long stems.

Scrophularia (Scrophulariaceae)
Figwort
Although there are almost 200 species
in this widely distributed genus of
temperate and subtropical plants,
mainly from the northern hemisphere,
only one species is used by the water
gardener for planting in shallow water.
Propagation: By division in spring.
Hardiness: Hardy to half hardy.

Thalia dealbata

Scrophularia auriculata 'Variegata'
Water figwort
This is an evergreen, clump-forming, hardy perennial, with stiff square stems. The nettle-like leaves have creamy margins and light green centres; smaller leaves are almost entirely cream. Spikes of insignificant, greenish-purple flowers are held above the foliage and much appreciated by bees.
Cultivation: Grow in full sun in water no deeper than 8cm (3in).
Height: 1m (3ft); *spread:* 60cm (2ft).

Sparganium (Sparganiaceae)
Burr weed
There are 21 mainly temperate species in this genus. They are found throughout the northern hemisphere, where they are common on the edges of large lakes, forming clumps in association with reeds and reedmaces. They are valuable plants for waterfowl, which use them as nesting sites and winter food.
Propagation: By seed or by division in spring.
Hardiness: Hardy.

Sparganium erectum (syn. S. ramosum)
This species, which is native to Europe and Asia, has rhizomatous roots that have strong pointed tips and bear rosettes of long, sword-shaped leaves, which are triangular at the base. In summer erect, unbranched flower spikes bear densely packed round, greenish-brown flowerheads, which are followed by prickly brown fruit.
Cultivation: Grow in full sun in water to 45cm (18in) deep.
Height: 1.5m (5ft); *spread:* indefinite.

Thalia (Marantaceae)
The genus contains 12 swamp-loving species from tropical and subtropical America and Africa. One or two species make striking specimens for the waterside of tropical pools.
Propagation: Mainly by seed, but large clumps can be divided in spring.
Hardiness: Half hardy to frost tender.

Thalia dealbata
This architecturally striking plant is tender. It has long, thick, glaucous blue leaves dusted with a white powder. Carried high above the leaves are the unusual small violet flowers. In temperate areas it makes an excellent conservatory plant.
Cultivation: Grow in full sun in 30–45cm (12–18in) of water.
Height: 1.8–3m (6–10ft); *spread:* 1.8m (6ft).

Typha minima

Typha (Typhaceae)
Reedmace, cat's tail
The genus contains ten species of cosmopolitan marsh-loving plants. They should be introduced with caution, however, because most species are extremely invasive and are capable of puncturing pool liners with the needlelike tips of their extensive rhizomes. The brown, poker-like flower-heads make popular dried flowers.
Propagation: By division of the rootstock in spring.
Hardiness: Hardy.

Typha angustifolia
Lesser reedmace, narrow-leaved cat's tail
This hardy species has slender, dark green leaves. The characteristic brown flower spikes are held above the leaves, with the male and female flowers separated by a gap of about 2.5cm (1in).
Cultivation: Grow in full sun. They will tolerate a water depth of up to 45cm (18in).
Height: 1.5m (5ft); *spread:* indefinite.

Typha laxmannii (syn. T. stenophylla)
Graceful cat's tail
This species is more elegant and slightly less invasive than *T. angustifolia.* It has greyish-green, half-round leaves, which are grooved on one side.
Cultivation: Grow in full sun in water to 30cm (12in) deep.
Height: 1.2–1.5m (4–5ft); *spread:* indefinite.

Typha minima
This small species is suitable for even the smallest pool. The leaves are needlelike, and the dark brown flower spikes are round.
Cultivation: Grow in full sun in water 8–10cm (3–4in) deep.
Height: 30–45cm (12–18in); *spread:* 60cm (2ft).

Veronica (Scrophulariaceae)
Speedwell
The large variable genus contains about 250 species, mainly from the northern hemisphere, which include a few hardy marginals.
Propagation: By softwood cuttings from the young growth in summer.
Hardiness: Hardy to frost hardy.

Veronica beccabunga
Brooklime
This is a hardy species, bearing spikes of dark blue flowers with white centres and glossy, rounded, fleshy leaves, which grow from cylindrical, hollow stems. It is an excellent plant for covering muddy banks.
Cultivation: Grow in full sun in water no more than 8cm (3in) deep.
Height: 30cm (12in); *spread:* indefinite.

Zantedeschia (Araceae)
A genus of six tender South African species, these are marsh-loving plants with thick rhizomes and arrow-shaped leaves, often with white, transparent dots. Many hybrids have been developed as decorative container plants.
Propagation: By seed or division in spring.
Hardiness: Hardy to frost tender.

Zantedeschia aethiopica (syn. Calla aethiopica)
Arum lily
This is the familiar florist's arum lily which can also be grown in the water garden as a tender marginal aquatic. It makes a distinctive specimen plant, forming a clump of arrow-shaped, glossy green leaves. From late spring to midsummer it produces the striking, exotic-looking, white flowers with yellow centres.
Cultivation: Grow in full sun or partial shade. In temperate areas it requires protection from cold winds and frost; submerge the plants in 30cm (12in) of water in winter in order to protect them in cold areas.
Height: 60cm–1m (2–3ft); *spread:* 60cm (2ft).

Zantedeschia aethiopica 'Crowborough'
This cultivar is the hardiest of the arum lilies and for this reason it is highly recommended for growing in colder positions. It is a truly striking sight if it is planted in groups, particularly in the margins of an informal pool.
Cultivation: Grow in sun or partial shade in 15cm (6in) of water.
Height: 60cm (2ft); *spread:* 45cm (18in).

Zantedeschia aethiopica 'Green Goddess'
An interesting frost-hardy cultivar, this has white flowers, which are heavily flushed with green.
Cultivation: Grow in full sun in moist soil or shallow margins where the covering of water is no more than 2.5–5cm (1–2in).
Height: 70cm (28in); *spread:* 23cm (9in).

Veronica beccabunga

Zantedeschia aethiopica 'Crowborough'

MOISTURE-LOVING PLANTS

The water's surface forms only one part of the water garden, and beyond the actual margins of the pool where the soil becomes moist, but is not saturated, there is a huge canvas on which to compose a setting for the water. There is a wide range of plants that are ideally suited to this moist zone, ranging in size from trees to tiny carpeting plants. The art of planting this area is to make it appear as much a part of the water garden as the waterlilies. Whereas many marginals may survive in this drier regime, moisture-lovers cannot cross into the saturated soil where the lack of oxygen will kill the roots. With ample moisture, however, the plants will grow quickly, and restraint is necessary in the density of planting in the same way as for the shallow-water plants because they quickly become overgrown.

Achillea (Asteraceae)
Yarrow
The genus contains about 85 temperate species from Europe, western Asia and North America. Although most species prefer a drier soil, *A. ptarmica* thrives in the moist soil by the water's edge.
Propagation: By division.
Hardiness: Hardy.

Achillea ptarmica
Sneezewort
This invasive perennial has strong stems with narrow, toothed, lance-shaped, dark green leaves. The loose, white flower-heads, 2–10cm (¾–4in) across, appear from early to late summer. 'Unschuld' is also white.
Cultivation: Grow in full sun in moist, well-drained soil.
Height: 60–90cm (2–3ft); *spread:* 60cm (2ft).

Aconitum (Ranunculaceae)
Aconite, monkshood, helmet flower, wolfsbane
A genus of about 100 temperate species from Europe, Asia and North America, which are found mainly on grassland and scrub. Certain species look particularly beautiful when they are massed by the waterside where

Achillea ptarmica 'Unschuld'

their flowers become exceptionally large. It is important to note that all aconites are poisonous.
Propagation: By seed or by division.
Hardiness: Hardy.

Aconitum napellus
Helmet flower, turk's cap, friar's cap.
This erect, hardy perennial has rounded, deeply lobed, dark green leaves, with the lobes further divided. The navy blue flowers are borne in dense spikes in midsummer.
Cultivation: Grow in full sun in moist soil.
Height: 1.2m (4ft); *spread:* 30cm (12in).

Aconitum napellus

Ajuga (Lamiaceae)
Bugle
This is a genus of 40 temperate and subtropical perennial creeping plants, which thrive in the damp soil by streams and informal pools.
Propagation: By division or by separating root stems.
Hardiness: Hardy.

Ajuga reptans
This creeping perennial, which can become invasive, is a good ground-cover plant. It has dark green, oblong to spoon-shaped leaves, 5–8cm (2–3in) long. Dark blue flowers are held in short spikes, 15cm (6in) tall, in late spring and early summer. Several cultivars have colourful leaves.
Cultivation: Grow in any moist soil in partial shade because the foliage will scorch in full sun.
Height: 15–20cm (6–8in); *spread:* indefinite.

Alchemilla (Rosaceae)
Lady's mantle
This is a large genus of about 300 hardy temperate species from Europe, Asia and America. They have a wide variety of uses and are particularly attractive when ample moisture allows them to reach their full potential.
Propagation: By seed or by division of large clumps.
Hardiness: Hardy to frost hardy.

Alchemilla mollis
This hardy perennial has roundish, downy leaves, 10–13cm (4–5in) across. The tiny flowers are yellowish-green and held in feathery sprays in early summer. Deadhead after flowering to prevent self-sowing.
Cultivation: Grow in full sun or partial shade in rich, moist soil.
Height: 45cm (18in); *spread:* 75cm (30in).

Anagallis (Primulaceae)
Pimpernel
This is a widely distributed genus of 20 species of small herbs, found in bogs, meadows and dry sites around the Mediterranean and in western Europe. *A. tenella* is especially suitable for moist, almost boggy, sites.
Propagation: By seed.
Hardiness: Hardy to frost hardy.

Anagallis tenella
Bog pimpernel
This hardy perennial has creeping masses of small, light green, roundish leaves. Small, pink, scented, bell-shaped flowers appear in midsummer.
Cultivation: Grow in full sun in moist, well-drained soil.
Height: 5–10cm (2–4in); *spread:* 40cm (16in).

Alchemilla mollis

Anagallis tenella

Angelica (Apiaceae)
This is a genus of 50 temperate species from damp woodland, fens and stream banks in the northern hemisphere. They are generally large, architectural plants, which look well as specimens in an informal woodland water garden.
Propagation: By seed.
Hardiness: Hardy.

Angelica archangelica
Garden angelica, archangel
A statuesque addition to the water garden, this hardy perennial has large, deeply indented leaves, carried on thick stems. The small, cream-white flowers are clustered together in large, round umbels, 25cm (10in) across, on short ribbed flower stems.
Cultivation: Grow in full or partial shade in deep, rich soil.
Height: 1.8m (6ft); *spread:* 1.2m (4ft).

Arum (Araceae)
A genus of 26 species of tuberous perennials, flowering mainly in the spring, these plants are native to shaded habitats in southern Europe, northern Africa and western Asia.
Propagation: By seed in spring.
Hardiness: Hardy to half hardy.

Arum italicum
This hardy perennial has attractive, arrow-shaped, green leaves, marked with white veins and up to 35cm (14in) long, which appear from late winter until early summer. The flowers are greenish-white spathes, 15–40cm (6–16in) long, and they are followed by columns of vermilion berries on stout stalks.
Cultivation: Grow in partial shade in rich, well-drained soil.
Height: 30cm (12in); *spread:* 15cm (6in).

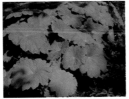
Astilboides tabularis

Arundo (Poaceae)
A genus of three reedy grasses from the warmer parts of the Old World. These decorative grasses carry large, feathery flower spikes and make distinctive specimen plants in containers in temperate areas so that they can be moved under cover in winter.
Propagation: By seed.
Hardiness: Half hardy.

Arundo donax
Giant reed
Although this magnificent plant can grow to 6m (20ft) in its natural habitat, it usually reaches only about 3m (10ft) in the colder parts of North America and Britain. It is grown for its attractive, bamboo-like foliage on thick, jointed stems and its large flower spikes, which are reddish at first, later turning white.
Cultivation: Grow in full sun, out of strong winds; protect in winter.
Height: 6m (20ft); *spread:* 1.5m (5ft).

Arundo donax var. *versicolor* (syn. *A. donax* 'Variegata')
This is smaller and less hardy than the species. The leaves are attractively striped with green and ivory-white.
Cultivation: Grow in full sun and give protection in winter.
Height: 1.8m (6ft); *spread:* 60cm (2ft).

Astrantia major subsp. *involucrata* 'Shaggy'

Astilbe (Saxifragaceae)
The genus contains about 12 temperate perennial species, originating from North America and S. E. Asia, and includes both tall and dwarf, handsome, herbaceous perennials. These make a colourful contribution to waterside planting. Their attractive foliage provides good undergrowth from which rise tapering, feathery spikes of white, crimson or pink flowers. The dry flower-heads are a rusty shade of brown, and provide an additional bonus in the autumn and winter if they are left on the plant.
Propagation: By division in early spring.
Hardiness: Hardy.

Astilbe × *arendsii*
This group contains many garden hybrids with a tremendous range of colours and foliage characteristics. They grow to 50–120cm (20–48in) tall. 'Elizabeth Bloom' is pale pink, while 'Fanal' has deep crimson flowers and dark green foliage.
Cultivation: Grow in sun or partial shade in moist, rich soil.
Height: 50–120cm (20–48in); *spread:* 20–90cm (8–36in).

Astilbe simplicifolia
This dwarf species from Japan bears short, attractively arched panicles of creamy coloured flowers above glossy foliage.
Cultivation: Grow in sun or partial shade in moist, rich soil.
Height and spread: 20cm (8in).

Astilboides (Saxifragaceae)
The single species in this genus is a moisture-loving perennial herb from woodland habitats in northern China. It thrives in shady, temperate gardens.
Propagation: By seed.
Hardiness: Hardy.

Astilboides tabularis (syn. *Rodgersia tabularis*)
This distinctive species has almost round, lotus-like, pale green leaves, borne on a central leaf stalk. The creamy white, clustered flowers are held above the leaves on strong stems.
Cultivation: Grow in shade in cool, moist soil and sheltered from wind.
Height: 1m (3ft); *spread:* 1.2m (4ft).

Astrantia (Apiaceae)
Hattie's pincushion, masterwort
The genus contains about 10 species of perennials, native to alpine woods and meadows of Europe and Asia.
Propagation: By seed or by division in spring.
Hardiness: Hardy.

Astrantia major
Greater masterwort
This European species bears five-lobed leaves in basal rosettes and erect umbels of small, five-petalled pink and green flowers, which are surrounded by bracts. *A. major* subsp. *involucrata* 'Shaggy' has white flowers and long, green-tipped bracts.
Cultivation: Grow in partial shade in rich, moist soil.
Height: 60cm (2ft); *spread:* 45cm (18in).

Arum italicum 'Pictum'

Astilbe 'Elizabeth Bloom'

Cardamine (Brassicaceae)
Bittercress
The genus contains 150 species of annuals and perennials, which mainly originate from the cool regions of the northern hemisphere. Some species in this genus become invasive weeds, so care must be taken.
Propagation: By seed.
Hardiness: Hardy.

Cardamine pratensis
Lady's smock, cuckoo flower, mayflower, meadow cress
The rosy-lilac flowers grow above cress-like leaves in late spring. It seeds itself easily when happy and makes an excellent plant for the fringes of the wildlife pool, where it can be successfully naturalized in long grass.
Cultivation: Grow in full or partial shade in rich soil.
Height: 30–50cm (12–20in); *spread:* 30cm (12in).

Cardamine pratensis 'Flore Pleno'
The double form is a more showy plant than the species. It has rosettes of cress-like leaves and masses of small, double, pale lilac flowers about 23–30cm (9–12in) tall. Being double flowered, it is unable to seed itself, but it spreads by the leaves taking root and developing new plantlets.
Cultivation: Grow in full or partial shade in rich soil.
Height: 20cm (8in); *spread:* 30cm (12in).

Cimicifuga (Ranunculaceae)
Bugbane, cohosh
The genus includes about 15 showy perennial species from Europe, central and eastern Asia and North America, where they are found in moist, shady grassland, woodland or scrub. The common name of bugbane owes its origin to the plant's traditional use to deter fleas.
Propagation: By seed.
Hardiness: Hardy.

Cimicifuga simplex
Flowering in late summer or early autumn, this clump-forming perennial has narrow spires of pure white, bottlebrush-like flowers. The plant has attractive, deeply divided leaves held on wiry stems, which, despite their fragile appearance, are extremely strong.
Cultivation: Grow in partial shade in fertile soil.
Height: 1.8m (6ft); *spread:* 60cm (2ft).

Cardamine pratensis

Crocosmia 'Lucifer'

Cimicifuga simplex var. *simplex* 'Brunette'
This is a very striking cultivar which has purplish-black leaves and compact flower spikes. These grow to a length of 20cm (8in). This cultivar has purple-tinted, off-white flowers.
Cultivation: Grow in partial shade in fertile soil.
Height: 1.2m (4ft); *spread:* 60cm (2ft).

Crocosmia (Iridaceae)
Montbretia
The seven species of this genus are clump-forming, mainly hardy perennials, which are native to South Africa. They have long, narrow leaves, rather similar to those of *Iris*, and they make a very striking display in late summer when their mainly red or orange flowers appear.
Propagation: By seed or by dividing thick clumps in spring.
Hardiness: Hardy to frost hardy.

Crocosmia × *curtonus*
This forms a strong, upright clump of pleated mid-green leaves with bright tomato-red flowers nearly 5cm (2in) long on slightly arching, sparsely branched spikes in midsummer.
Cultivation: Grow in full sun or partial shade.
Height: 1–1.2m (3–4ft); *spread:* 15cm (6in).

Crocosmia 'Lucifer'
Another cultivar with upright flowers which are a bright tomato-red colour, 5cm (2in) long in bold, slightly arching spikes during midsummer.
Cultivation: Sun or partial shade.
Height: 1–1.2m (3–4ft); *spread:* 30cm (12in) or more.

Crocosmia masoniorum
This species differs from the other crocosmias because its arching flower stems hold vermilion or orange flowers upright instead of facing forwards under the stem. The sword-shaped, dark green leaves turn a warm beige as they fade.
Cultivation: Grow in full sun or partial shade.
Height: 1m (3ft); *spread:* 8cm (3in).

Darmera (Saxifragaceae)
Formerly known as *Peltiphyllum*, this is a North American genus, containing a single species. It makes a versatile plant for the waterside, tolerating a wide range of conditions of varying degrees of moisture.
Propagation: By seed or by division in spring.
Hardiness: Hardy.

Darmera peltata (syn. *Peltiphyllum peltatum*)
Umbrella plant, Indian rhubarb
This hardy perennial will make a bold statement at the edge of a pool, where its large round leaves can be reflected in the water. In early spring, before the leaves appear, it produces small, starry, pink flowers, which are borne in rounded heads on slender, red-tinted stalks, 30–60cm (1–2ft) long. The leaves appear in mid-spring, after the frosts and, like the flowers, are held well above the ground on slender stalks. The common name derives from the shape of the leaves, which form large, deep green, heavily veined plates, deeply lobed and coarsely toothed, nearly 60cm (2ft) in diameter and turning beautiful shades of red in autumn. The roots form thick surface rhizomes, which are extremely useful for stabilizing the muddy banks of a pond.

Cimicifuga simplex

Darmera peltata

Cultivation: Grow in a sheltered position in muddy, almost saturated soil in full sun or partial shade. Do not grow where water covers the roots. *Height:* 1–1.8m (3–6ft); *spread:* 1m (3ft) or more.

Dodecatheon
(Primulaceae)
American cowslip
The genus contains 14 hardy perennial species from North America, ranging from damp valleys in the prairies to the Rocky Mountains. All the species closely resemble one another but vary in height. They become dormant in the summer after flowering and make good subjects for rocky slopes near a stream.
Propagation: By seed or divide large clumps in spring.
Hardiness: Hardy.

Dodecatheon meadia
(syn. *D. pauciflorum*)
Shooting star
This species has distinctive rose-magenta, cyclamen-like flowers, 1–2cm (½–¾in) long, borne on strong stems above a basal rosette of oval, toothed, pale to mid-green leaves 25cm (10in) long. After fertilization the flowers point upwards, giving it the common name of shooting star.
Cultivation: Grow in full sun or partial shade in a moist, fertile soil.
Height: 60cm (2ft); *spread:* 25cm (10in).

Eupatorium (Asteraceae)
Hemp agrimony
The genus contains about 40 species of hardy perennials, annuals and sub-shrubs, mostly from America,

Dodecatheon meadia

Eupatorium purpureum

with some from the Old World. They are large, rather coarse, easily grown plants which are only suitable for large gardens in damp soil near extensive informal or wildlife pools.
Propagation: By division in spring.
Hardiness: Hardy to frost tender.

Eupatorium cannabinum
This tall, clump-forming, hardy perennial bears pink, purple or white flowers in terminal clusters in late summer and early autumn. The downy leaves are 13cm (5in) across with coarsely toothed lobes. It is prone to wilting in strong sun if there is inadequate moisture at the root.
Cultivation: Grow in partial shade.
Height: 60cm–1.5m (2–5ft); *spread:* 1.2m (4ft).

Eupatorium purpureum
Joe-pye weed
A clump-forming, hardy perennial, this resembles *E. cannabinum* but is larger and more brightly coloured, with flat flowerheads, sometimes reaching 30cm (1ft) across, of fluffy, mauve-pink, upturned flowers on dark purplish stalks.
Cultivation: Grow in partial shade.
Height: 2.2m (7ft); *spread:* 1m (3ft).

Filipendula (Rosaceae)
This small genus of about 10 species of hardy perennials, similar to *Spiraea* and found in the Himalayas, northern Asia, Europe and North America, prefer mostly moist places. Most are suitable for planting in a woodland garden or damp meadows near a wildlife pool.
Propagation: By seed.
Hardiness: Hardy.

Filipendula ulmaria

Filipendula ulmaria
Queen of the meadow, meadowsweet
This is a clump-forming perennial which is excellent for the wildlife garden. It produces creamy flowers in dense corymbs, to 25cm (10in) across, above strong, erect stems bearing pinnate leaves, 5–10cm (2–4in) across, which are downy on the underside.
Cultivation: Grow in full sun or partial shade.
Height: 1–1.5m (3–5ft); *spread:* 60cm (2ft).

Gentiana (Gentianaceae)
The large genus contains about 400 species of annual or perennial plants, which are widely distributed across Europe, Asia, North and South America and New Zealand. The more familiar blue-flowered gentians are excellent for growing in rock

gardens, provided that the soil is acidic. There is one species, however, *G. asclepiadea*, which prefers moist conditions in woodland, where it associates particularly well with grasses and ferns.
Propagation: By seed.
Hardiness: Hardy.

Gentiana asclepiadea
Willow gentian
This plant, which is native to Europe, is a reliable and graceful plant, with narrow, willow-like leaves and rich blue flowers, which are arranged in axillary clusters around the upper half of the stem.
Cultivation: Grow in deep moist soil and plenty of shade.
Height: 30–60cm (1–2ft); *spread:* 45cm (18in).

Geum (Rosaceae)
A genus of about 50 species of rhizomatous perennials, which are widely distributed throughout the world, especially in cold and temperate regions. They can be grown as border or rock plants, and some species are ideal in moist soil near an informal pool.
Propagation: By seed or by division in autumn or spring.
Hardiness: Hardy.

Geum rivale
Water avens
A lover of wet meadows and marshy places, water avens bears pendent, dull, purplish-pink flowers and straw-berry-like leaves. The reddish-brown sepals are almost as long as the petals.
Cultivation: Grow in full sun.
Height: 25–30cm (10–12in); *spread:* 60cm (2ft).

Gentiana asclepiadea

Gunnera manicata

Gunnera (Gunneraceae)

A genus of 40–50 species of slightly tender perennials, which are widely distributed in the southern hemisphere. Some of them are gigantic plants, producing huge leaves, and they can be grown outside in temperate areas. Plenty of moisture and protection from wind is needed if they are to be seen at their best. Cover the crowns in winter with the dead leaves as soon as they are frosted.
Propagation: By seed.
Hardiness: Hardy to frost hardy.

Gunnera magellanica

This is a tiny, mat-forming herbaceous perennial. The dark green, rounded to kidney-shaped leaves grow to 6cm (2½in) across and are tinged bronze when young.
Cultivation: Grow in sun or partial shade.
Height: 8–15cm (3–6in); *spread:* 30cm (12in) or more.

Gunnera manicata (syn. G. brasiliensis)

Giant rhubarb
This is the largest species of *Gunnera*, with prickly stems 1.8m (6ft) tall and vast leaves, to 1.8m (6ft) across, that are harsh, bristly and deeply lobed. The curious flower spike is like a huge bottlebrush, 30cm–1m (1–3ft) tall, tinged with red. It grows from a very thick root covered in brown papery scales that look like fur. It is spectacular when reflected in water.
Cultivation: Grow in sun or partial shade.
Height: 2.4m (8ft); *spread:* 4m (13ft).

Hemerocallis (Hemerocallidaceae)

Daylily
This genus contains about 15 species of herbaceous perennials from eastern Asia, and they provide a colourful contribution to the sides of a water garden. The individual flowers last for only one day but are produced in a long succession. There are countless cultivars available, many of which are improved dwarf strains suitable for the smaller garden.
Propagation: By division in spring.
Hardiness: Hardy to frost hardy.

Hemerocallis cultivars

There are more than 30,000 named cultivars of *Hemerocallis*, many of which are derived from *H. fulva* and *H. multiflora*. They are mostly clump-forming plants, with arching, strap-shaped, dark green leaves, usually 75–120cm (30–48in) long, but many dwarfer forms are now being introduced. The flowers are borne on erect stems over a long period, mainly from late spring to late summer. The flowers range in colour from almost white, through yellow and orange to dark purple and deepest red-black. *H.* 'Wind Song' is a semi-evergreen cultivar with wide leaves and creamy-yellow almost round flowers, 15cm (6in) across, on sturdy stems in early and midsummer.
Cultivation: Grow in full sun.
Height: 62cm–1m (25–36in); *spread:* 45cm–1m (18–36in).

Heracleum (Apiaceae)

The genus contains about 60 species of large biennial or perennial plants from northern temperate regions and some tropical mountain regions. They should be avoided by those susceptible to skin allergies.
Propagation: By seed.
Hardiness: Hardy.

Heracleum mantegazzianum

Giant cow parsnip, giant hogweed
A good subject for the waterside, this plant has large, basal, divided leaves, 1m (3ft) wide, and wheel-like heads of white flowers on stout hollow stems.
Cultivation: Grow in sun or partial shade.
Height: 2.4–3m (8–10ft); *spread:* 1.8m (6ft).

Hosta (Hostaceae)

This genus contains about 70 species of hardy, clump-forming, handsome herbaceous perennials, which are mainly native to eastern Asia, especially Japan. From these species numerous cultivars have been developed, and the naming is often somewhat confused. Their foliage is especially attractive

Hemerocallis 'Wind Song'

near the waterside, and although they can be grown in most soils, they are at their best in moist conditions.
Propagation: By division.
Hardiness: Hardy.

Hosta crispula

This has broadly lance- to heart-shaped leaves, wavy margined, 20–30cm (8–12in) long, tapering to twisted tips, and with irregular white margins. The flowers are lavender-white.
Cultivation: Grow in moist soil in full or partial shade.
Height: 80cm (32in); *spread:* 1m (3ft).

Hosta cultivars

H. 'Honeybells' grows to 75cm (30in) and spreads to 1.2m (4ft). It has pale-green, heart-shaped leaves, 28cm (11in) long, with strong vein markings, growing in an open mound shape. The bell-shaped flowers are white, occasionally lavender blue on stems reaching 1m (3ft) long in late summer. It should be grown in partial shade. 'Hadspen Blue' also prefers partial shade, and grows to 25cm (10in) high and spreads to 60cm (24in). This cultivar has thick, grey-blue, close-veined leaves, 13cm (5in) long. The bell-shaped, pale, grey-mauve flowers are held on purple-spotted flower spikes 35cm (14in) long. 'Sum and Substance', which can grow in sun or partial shade, grows to 75cm (30in) and spreads to 1.2m (4ft). This distinctive cultivar has heart-shaped glossy, yellow-green leaves, 50cm (20in)

Heracleum mantegazzianum

Hosta sieboldiana

long, which become puckered when mature. Very pale lilac bell-shaped flowers are produced in midsummer on stems 1m (3ft) long.
Cultivation: Grow in moist soil in full or partial shade.

Hosta fortunei
A vigorous species, this has heart-shaped, matt, dark green, wavy edged leaves, about 20cm (8in) long. It has the bonus of striking, pale lilac flowers that are carried well above the foliage.
Cultivation: Grow in moist soil in full or partial shade.
Height and spread: 80cm (32in).

Hosta lancifolia
This hosta forms a dense mound of arching, long-pointed, shining dark green leaves, 10–18cm (4–7in) long, making overlapping mounds, from which arise large, deep lilac, trumpet-shaped flowers on tall, slender stalks.
Cultivation: Grow in moist soil in full or partial shade.
Height: 60cm (2ft); *spread:* 75cm (30in).

Hosta plantaginea
This is one of the choicest, plain-foliaged species. It has beautiful, glossy, bright green, arching, heart-shaped leaves, 15–28cm (6–11in) long. The trumpet-like, marble white flowers are produced late in the season and have a delicate, lily-like fragrance. Unusually, this species prefers a sunny position.
Cultivation: Grow in moist soil in sun.
Height: 60cm (2ft); *spread:* 1m (3ft).

Hosta sieboldiana
This species produces the most dramatic leaves of all the hostas. The large, distinctly pointed, cordate leaves may vary in depth of colouring, being grey-green, bluish or glaucous and reaching a length of 35cm (14in). In early summer bell-shaped, pale lilac-grey flowers, which fade to white, are borne on stems 1m (3ft) long.
Cultivation: Grow in moist soil in full or partial shade.
Height: 80cm (32in); *spread:* 1.2m (4ft).

Hosta undulata
This species has almost spirally twisted, pointed leaves, to 9cm (3½in) wide, with bold creamy-white variegation running lengthways down the leaf and dark green, undulating margins. Funnel-shaped mauve flowers are borne in early and midsummer.
Cultivation: Grow in moist soil in full or partial shade.
Height and spread: 45cm (18in).

Hosta ventricosa 'Variegata'
This variety has distinctive leaves which are irregularly margined with yellow and later turn creamy-white. Leafy flower stems, which grow to 80–100cm (32–40in) in height, bear tubular, bell-shaped, deep purple flowers in midsummer.
Cultivation: Grow in partial shade.
Height: 50cm (20in); *spread:* to 1m (3ft).

Inula
(Asteraceae/Compositae)
A genus of about 100 species of annuals, perennials and a few sub-shrubs found in temperate regions of Europe, Asia and America, these plants are characterized by their large, flat, daisy-like flower-heads. They make ideal plants for the wild garden.
Propagation: By division in autumn or spring.
Hardiness: Hardy to frost hardy.

Inula magnifica
This is a giant hardy perennial, which requires ample space to be appreciated. The enormous, broad, dock-like leaves have a rough matt texture, and they make a large mound at the base of the plant, becoming smaller as they climb the brown stems. At the tips of the stems, brown buds open to large, vivid deep yellow, fine-rayed daisies, 13–15cm (5–6in) across.
Cultivation: Grow in full sun.
Height: 1.8m (6ft); *spread:* 1m (3ft).

Inula magnifica

Iris (Iridaceae)
The genus contains about 300 species of herbaceous perennials from a wide range of habitats in the northern hemisphere. Irises are synonymous with water gardens, and a careful selection of forms will provide a lengthy flowering season. Three species suitable for the margins of a pool are described in the section on marginals.
Propagation: Those suitable for the moist areas near water are propagated by division.
Hardiness: Hardy to frost tender.

Iris chrysographes
A native of western China, this species has grassy leaves and flowers that are rich velvety purple with golden-yellow etched veins.
Cultivation: Grow in full sun.
Height and spread: 60cm (2ft).

Iris ensata (syn. I. kaempferi)
Japanese water iris
These clematis-flowered irises from Japan range in colour from white to shades of pink, lavender, blue, violet, yellow and crimson; some are plain and others have bold and elaborate markings on the petals. The leaves are 20–60cm (8–24in) long with a prominent midrib. They can flourish in shallow water during the summer but must not be waterlogged in the winter. They are the most exotic of all the irises, with their butterfly-like flowers, which are held horizontally, providing an unequalled show of colour.
Cultivation: Grow in full sun.
Height: 1m (3ft); *spread:* 30cm (1ft).

Iris fulva
Louisiana iris
Originating in the southern United States, these irises have strap-shaped, bright green leaves, arching at the tips. The slender, slightly zigzag stems bear from four to six copper or orange-red flowers, 6–7cm (2½–3in) across, in late spring.
Cultivation: Grow in full sun.
Height and spread: 60cm (2ft).

Iris sibirica
Siberian iris
Native to Europe and northern Asia, this iris has grass-like leaves, to 45cm (18in) long. Slender, branching heads of violet-blue flowers are produced in early summer, with the fall petals marked with an area of yellow or white veining in the centre. The narrow, shining, chestnut-brown seed-heads are an added attraction.
Cultivation: Grow in full sun.
Height: 1m (3ft); *spread:* indefinite.

Hosta ventricosa

Hosta ventricosa 'Variegata'

Iris sibirica

Leucojum aestivum

Lobelia cardinalis

Leucojum
(Amaryllidaceae)
Snowflake
The genus contains nine or ten species of bulbous plants originating from central Europe and the Mediterranean region. The green-tipped, white flowers resemble large snowdrops.
Propagation: By seed or by removing offsets from around the bulb once the leaves have died down.
Hardiness: Hardy to frost hardy.

Leucojum aestivum
Summer snowflake
This species looks spectacular when it is planted in large clumps by the waterside. It produces glossy, daffodil-like leaves of richest green and sturdy green stems, supporting bell-shaped white flowers with each outer petal tipped in green.
Cultivation: Grow in full sun.
Height: 30–60cm (1–2ft); *spread:* 8cm (3in).

Leucojum vernum
Spring snowflake
This delightful little spring-flowering species has strap-shaped, semi-erect, green basal leaves. Leafless stems bear one or two pendent, bell-shaped, fragrant flowers with six white petals tipped with green.
Cultivation: Grow in full sun.
Height: 20–30cm (8–12in); *spread:* 8cm (3in).

Ligularia (Asteraceae)
This is a large genus, containing about 180 species of herbaceous, moisture-loving perennials, which are native to the Old World, north of the tropics. They are imposing,

statuesque waterside plants, which can either be grown in striking groups or, alternatively, treated as specimen planting.
Propagation: By seed or by dividing in spring or after flowering.
Hardiness: Hardy.

Ligularia dentata 'Desdemona'
Rounded, brownish green leaves with a deep maroon-purple underside form a basal cluster below deep orange flower-heads.
Cultivation: Partial shade is better as the leaves are prone to wilting in strong sun.
Height and spread: to 1m (3ft).

Ligularia 'Gregynog Gold'
This is an excellent choice for the smaller water garden, where most of the ligularias would be too tall. This variety has handsome, richly veined, heart-shaped leaves, growing to 35cm (14in) long, and huge, conical spires of large, vivid orange-yellow flowers.
Cultivation: Grow in full sun or partial shade.
Height: 1–1.2m (3–4ft); *spread:* 1m (3ft).

Ligularia przewalskii (syn. Senecio przewalskii)
This species has very finely cut, dark green leaves, to 30cm (12in) long. The leaves resemble fingers and are borne on nearly black stems that bear a spire of small, yellow daisy-like flowers.
Cultivation: Grow in partial shade. It will wilt easily in bright light if the soil is not kept moist.
Height: 1.5–1.8 (5–6ft); *spread:* 1m (3ft).

Ligularia dentata 'Desdemona'

Lobelia (Campanulaceae)
This genus of more than 350 species of annual and perennial plants is found in tropical and temperate regions, especially the Americas. The perennial species are elegant and brightly coloured waterside plants, which look stunning when planted in groups. Although ample moisture is required in the summer, they should not be too wet in the winter.
Propagation: By seed; take cuttings of *L. cardinalis* in summer.
Hardiness: Hardy to frost tender.

Lobelia cardinalis
Cardinal flower
This striking species is native to North America, and it is a clump-forming, rather short-lived, frost hardy rhizomatous perennial. The lance-shaped leaves make a basal rosette and may vary in colour from fresh green to red-bronze. Leafy stems support strong spikes of intensely vivid, scarlet-lipped flowers in late summer.
Cultivation: Grow in full sun.
Height: 1m (3ft); *spread:* 30cm (1ft).

Lobelia × gerardii 'Vedrariensis'
This is a reliable frost hardy perennial with basal rosettes of lance-shaped, dark green leaves, 10cm (4in) long, often with a reddish tinge. Stout stems bear racemes of long-lasting, rich violet flowers throughout the summer.
Cultivation: Grow in full sun.
Height: 1m (3ft); *spread:* 30cm (1ft).

Lobelia siphilitica
Blue cardinal flower
Native to the eastern United States, this clump-forming, hardy perennial bears erect stems with whorls of crinkly light green leaves on the lower part and blue, two-lipped flowers at the top.
Cultivation: Grow in partial or full shade.
Height: 60cm (2ft); *spread:* 30cm (1ft).

Lobelia × speciosa
This hybrid closely resembles *L. cardinalis* but is not so hardy. It has deeper and showier flowers and deep maroon leaves. There are numerous and beautiful cultivars, such as *L.* 'Queen Victoria' and *L.* 'Bees' Flame', both of which have dazzling, large, velvety, scarlet flowers and crimson-maroon leaves.
Cultivation: Grow in full sun or partial shade.
Height: 1m (3ft); *spread:* 50cm (20in).

Lychnis (Caryophyllaceae)
Catchfly, campion
The genus contains between 15 and 20 species of biennials and perennials, which are found in a wide range of habitats in northern temperate regions. One species makes a charming waterside plant for the wildlife pool.
Propagation: By seed.
Hardiness: Hardy.

Lychnis flos-cuculi

Lychnis flos-cuculi
Ragged robin
Native to Europe, this species flowers in spring, bearing star-shaped, pale to bright purplish-pink flowers with deeply cut petals. The flowers are sparsely produced on loose stems.
Cultivation: Grow in full sun.
Height: 30–60cm (1–2ft); *spread:* 80cm (32in).

Lysimachia
(Primulaceae)
Loosestrife
A genus of 150 species of mostly herbaceous perennials, found throughout the world in temperate and subtropical regions. Larger species are suitable for moist mixed borders or bog gardens. Low-growing species provide ground cover in muddy soil.
Propagation: By seed or by division in spring or autumn.
Hardiness: Hardy to frost tender.

Lysimachia nummularia
Creeping Jenny
Originating in central Europe, this hardy creeping plant is useful for carpeting edges by the waterside. The small, rounded, green leaves hug the ground. In early summer bright yellow, cupped, upturned flowers, 2cm (¾in) across, are borne along the stems. The yellow-leaved cultivar, *L. nummularia* 'Aurea', is preferable to the green-leaved species.
Cultivation: Grow in full sun.
Height: 5cm (2in); *spread:* indefinite.

Lythrum (Lythraceae)
Loosestrife
There are about 38 species of hardy herbaceous plants and small shrubs in the genus. They are found in damp

Lythrum salicaria

places throughout the temperate regions and are ideal for mass planting in wild garden settings where there is plenty of moisture. They are extremely invasive, and the planting of some species is prohibited in many areas of the United States.
Propagation: By seed or by division in spring.
Hardiness: Hardy.

Lythrum salicaria
Purple loosestrife
This tall, leafy, clump-forming perennial has erect, stiff stems bearing lance-shaped, downy leaves, 10cm (4in) long. It produces tall, slender spires, 45cm (18in) long, of star-shaped, bright purple-red to purple-pink flowers from midsummer to early autumn.
Cultivation: Grow in full sun.
Height: 1.2m (4ft); *spread:* 45cm (18in) or more.

Lythrum salicaria 'Feuerkerze' (syn. L. salicaria 'Firecandle')
This is a slightly more compact cultivar, bearing intense rose-red flowers.
Cultivation: Grow in full sun.
Height: 1m (3ft); *spread:* 45cm (18in).

Macleaya (Papaveraceae)
Plume poppy
There are three species from China and Japan in this genus of large herbaceous plants with handsome leaves. They thrive in moist but well-drained soil.
Propagation: By seed or by division.
Hardiness: Hardy.

Macleaya cordata
A hardy perennial, this has grey to olive-green leaves with rounded, toothed lobes, which are white-downy

Macleaya cordata

Persicaria cuspidatum

beneath. Large, plume-like panicles of pendent buff-white flowers are borne on grey-green stems in midsummer.
Cultivation: Grow in full sun.
Height: 1.5–2.2m (5–7ft); *spread:* 1m (3ft).

Persicaria
(Polygonaceae)
This genus contains between 50 and 80 species of annual and perennial herbs, mainly from temperate regions around the world, which grow in the moist soils near pools and streams. They range in size from large, thicket-like canes to low-spreading, ground-cover plants.
Propagation: By division of the perennial species.
Hardiness: Hardy to half hardy.

Persicaria amplexicaulis (syn. Polygonum amplexicaule)
This hardy plant has a long-lasting display of spiky flowers from midsummer to autumn. It makes lush, leafy growth in moist soils, producing lance-shaped, mid-green leaves, 25cm (10in) long. The sprawling growth culminates in thin spikes of vivid crimson flowers.
Cultivation: Grow in full sun or partial shade.
Height and spread: 1.2m (4ft).

Persicaria bistorta (syn. Polygonum bistorta)
Snakeweed, bistort
This vigorous, hardy plant has clusters of basal leaves, 8–15cm (3–6in) long, that are oval, pointed and boldly veined. The flowers form erect, broad, pink spikes, 5–8cm (2–3in) long.
Cultivation: Grow in full sun.
Height: 80cm (32in); *spread:* 1m (3ft).

Persicaria bistorta 'Superba'

Persicaria bistorta 'Superba'
This hardy cultivar produces fat pokers of densely packed flowers of soft mauve-pink in midsummer above large, dock-like leaves.
Cultivation: Grow in full sun.
Height and spread: 1m (3ft).

Persicaria cuspidatum
Originating from Japan, Korea and China, this hardy, vigorous species grows on damp hillsides. It is ideal for a large garden where its spreading roots have ample room. It has several stems clothed with large, pale green, oval leaves, which hang over small chains of creamy green flowers.
Cultivation: Grow in sun or shade.
Height: 1.5–2.25m (5–7ft); *spread:* indefinite.

Petasites (Asteraceae)
Butterbur, sweet coltsfoot
The genus contains 14 to 15 species of moisture-loving perennials with invasive rhizomes from Europe, Asia and North America. The round leaves are effective but can be a nuisance once established.
Propagation: By division in spring and autumn.
Hardiness: Hardy to frost hardy.

Petasites fragrans

Petasites fragrans
Winter heliotrope
Native to Europe, this is one of the earliest flowering plants for the waterside, providing valuable early nectar for bees. From late winter to early spring the almond-scented clusters of starry, pale lilac flowers, which grow to 1cm (½in) across, are surrounded by large, rounded, light green leaves, 15–20cm (6–8in) in diameter. This is not reliably hardy, but the rhizome may survive below ground, even if the top growth is damaged by frost.
Cultivation: Grow in partial or full shade.
Height: 30cm (1ft); *spread:* 1.5m (5ft).

Phormium (Agavaceae)
Flax lily
The genus contains two species from New Zealand. They are exceptionally striking plants, providing strong architectural features in damp soil provided there is adequate drainage in winter. They make good plants for coastal gardens.
Propagation: By seed or by division in spring.
Hardiness: Borderline hardy.

Phormium tenax
New Zealand flax
This impressive plant has rigid, upright leaves, to 3m (10ft) long, which are dark green above and blue-green beneath. The stout flower stems grow above the foliage and support dull red, tubular flowers in a spike, which are followed by long-lasting, curved seed pods.
Cultivation: Grow in full sun.
Height: 3.6m (12ft); *spread:* 1.8m (6ft).

Primula (Primulaceae)
The large genus contains around 400 species, mainly from northern temperate regions. Many species are suited to the moist soil by streams and informal pools, where they provide a vivid display in late spring and early summer, particularly when they are massed into large groups.
Propagation: By seed as soon as ripe in late summer or by division in late summer or early autumn.
Hardiness: Unless specified, all those described here are hardy.

Primula alpicola
One of the many primulas from the Himalayas, this is native to Tibet. The toothed or scalloped elliptical leaves, 10cm (4in) long, form a rosette at the base of the plant. The pale yellow, white or violet, fragrant, tubular, drooping flowers are borne on mealy stems in umbels of 6–12 flowers.
Cultivation: Grow in partial shade.
Height: 15–50cm (6–20in); *spread:* 30cm (1ft).

Primula beesiana
This deciduous, sometimes evergreen, candelabra primula from China forms rosettes of leaves that die down in winter to basal buds or reduced rosettes. It has toothed, mid-green leaves with red midribs. White, mealy flower stems bear 2 to 8 whorls of yellow-eyed, reddish-pink flowers, 2cm (¾in) across.
Cultivation: Grow in partial shade.
Height: 23cm (9in); *spread:* 60cm (2ft).

Primula bulleyana
This Chinese candelabra primula is a rosette-forming species with toothed, mid-green, lance-shaped leaves,

which grow to 30cm (12in) in length. In early summer, stout stems bear 5 to 7 whorls of crimson flower buds which open to orange flowers.
Cultivation: Grow in partial shade.
Height and spread: 60cm (2ft).

Primula prolifera
This is a vigorous Chinese species. The spoon- to diamond-shaped basal leaves are finely toothed, deep green and to 35cm (14in) long. The candelabra flower spike bears from one to seven whorls of fragrant, white-mealy, pale to golden-yellow flowers, 2.5cm (1in) across.
Cultivation: Grow in partial shade.
Height: 1m (3ft); *spread:* 60cm (2ft).

Primula pulverulenta
Native to China, this is one of the most elegant candelabra primulas. The leaves are slightly smaller and more wrinkled than many of the other candelabra primulas, and the flowers are enhanced by the mealy farina on the flower stem. The tubular flowers are deep-red or red-purple, 2.5cm (1in) across, and are borne in early summer.
Cultivation: Grow in partial shade.
Height and spread: 60cm (2ft).

Primula rosea
Native to the Himalayas, this is one of the earliest to flower. The mid-green basal leaves, 20cm (8in) long, are lance-shaped, finely toothed and bronzed initially. They form rosettes and emerge after the flowers. The yellow-eyed, red-pink flowers, 2.5cm (1in) across, are produced in polyan-thus-like umbels.
Cultivation: Grow in partial shade.
Height: 15–23cm (6–9in); *spread:* 20cm (8in).

Phormium tenax

Primula sikkimensis
Himalayan cowslip
The lance-shaped, pale green leaves, 30cm (1ft) long, are toothed, shiny and grow in basal rosettes. The white-mealy, funnel-shaped, yellow or cream flowers, 2.5cm (1in) across, are produced in umbels in late spring.
Cultivation: Grow in partial shade.
Height: 60cm–1m (2–3ft); *spread:* 60cm (2ft).

Primula vialii
The flowers of this frost hardy Chinese species resemble tiny red-hot pokers. The basal, rosette-forming leaves have toothed edges and are hairy and broadly lance-shaped, growing to 30cm (12in) long. Stiff, stout, white-mealy stems support dense flower spikes, 15cm (6in) long, of small, tubular, blue-violet flowers in midsummer.
Cultivation: Grow in partial shade.
Height and spread: 30cm (1ft).

Primula bulleyana

Primula beesiana

Ranunculus ficaria 'Brazen Hussy'

Rheum palmatum

Rodgersia pinnata

Senecio smithii

Ranunculus
(Ranunculaceae)
There are approximately 400 species of temperate and tropical moisture-loving and aquatic plants in this large, cosmopolitan genus. Of these, almost 40 can be grown in water.
Propagation: By division in spring and summer.
Hardiness: Hardy to half hardy.

Ranunculus ficaria 'Brazen Hussy'
This is a hardy cultivar of the lesser celandine which produces glossy, deep chocolate-brown leaves and shining, golden yellow flowers with a bronze reverse. The heart-shaped leaves, 2–5cm (¾–2in) across, appear in early spring and die down after flowering.
Cultivation: Grow in sun or partial shade.
Height: 5cm (2in); *spread:* 30cm (12in).

Rheum (Polygonaceae)
Originating in Siberia, the Himalayas and eastern Asia, this genus includes about 50 species of strong perennial herbs which have thick, woody rhizomes. They resemble giant rhubarbs and are a superb choice for specimen planting by the side of the pool.
Propagation: By seed or by division in early spring.
Hardiness: Hardy.

Rheum alexandrae
From western China, this species is much smaller than most other rheums. It has rosettes of attractively veined, dark green, glossy leaves, 20cm (8in) across, with heart-shaped bases. In early summer the yellow-green flowers appear in spikes that are 60cm (2ft) long, with the flowers partially obscured by creamy coloured bracts, which highlight the spike even more.
Cultivation: Grow in full sun or partial shade.
Height: 1m (3ft); *spread:* 60cm (2ft).

Rheum palmatum
Chinese rhubarb
Native to China and Tibet, this is the most often grown species. It has huge, apple-green, rounded, palmately lobed and coarsely toothed leaves, growing 1m (3ft) long and with red undersides. In early summer, stems 1.8 (6ft) high carry panicles of masses of tiny, star-shaped, creamy-green to deep-red flowers.
Cultivation: Grow in full sun or partial shade.
Height: 1.8–2.4m (6–8ft); *spread:* 1.8m (6ft).

Rodgersia (Saxifragaceae)
The genus of six species of handsome, erect, herbaceous perennials is native to China and Japan. The plants thrive in moist peaty soils if they are sheltered from wind; they do very well in the woodland margins.
Propagation: By seed or by division in early spring.
Hardiness: Hardy.

Rodgersia aesculifolia
This clump-forming Chinese species has leaves like those of the horse chestnut. They are 25cm (10in) long, with densely woolly, red-brown stalks and veins. The numerous small white or pink flowers are star shaped and are borne in large panicles, to 60cm (2ft) long, which resemble astilbes.
Cultivation: Grow in full or partial shade.
Height: 1.2–1.5m (4–5ft); *spread:* 1m (3ft).

Rodgersia pinnata
Another Chinese species, this has pinnate, crinkled leaves, which are glossy and dark green, 90cm (36in) long, and heavily veined. Reddish-green stems bear star-shaped, yellowish-white, pink or red flowers in panicles that are 30–70cm (12–28in) long.
Cultivation: Grow in full or partial shade.
Height: 1.2m (4ft); *spread:* 75cm (30in).

Schizostylis (Iridaceae)
Kaffir lily
The single species in this genus is a temperate, bulbous-like herbaceous plant from South Africa. It is rather similar to the gladiolus and is an excellent choice for near the water's edge. They flower late into the autumn and extend the colours of the water garden with various cultivars in shades of orange and pink.
Propagation: by seed or division in the spring.
Hardiness: Borderline hardy.

Schizostylis coccinea
The species has long, sheathing, sword-shaped leaves, 40cm (16in) long, with distinct midribs. The scarlet flowers are open, cup-shaped, 2cm (¾in) across, and are held on spikes in the autumn.
Cultivation: Grow in full sun.
Height: 60cm (2ft); *spread:* 30cm (1ft).

Senecio
(Asteraceae)
The huge genus contains about 1,000 species, which are found throughout the world, mainly in mountain or temperate regions. Only one of these species is suitable for the moist soil of the informal temperate water garden, where it requires plenty of space to show off its handsome leaves and flowers.
Propagation: By division.
Hardiness: Hardy to frost tender.

Senecio smithii
Native to southern Chile and the Falkland Islands, this hardy herbaceous perennial has spear-shaped, coarsely serrated, dark green, leathery leaves, about 45cm (18in) long and 23cm (9in) across. The densely clustered flower-heads are composed of several yellow-eyed white daisies, each 2.5cm (1in) across.
Cultivation: Grow in full sun or partial shade.
Height: 1.2–1.5m (4–5ft); *spread:* 1m (3ft).

Trollius (Ranunculaceae)
Globeflower
There are about 30 species of hardy herbaceous perennials in this genus from Europe, Asia and North America. Compact in growth, they love moist soils. The profuse flowers of many species look like double buttercups.
Propagation: By seed or by division as soon as new growth begins or in autumn.
Hardiness: Hardy.

Trollius × *cultorum* cultivars
These cultivars have glossy basal leaves, 18cm (7in) long, which are divided into segments. Bowl-shaped flowers, 2.5–6cm (1–2½in) across, are borne from mid-spring to midsummer in various shades of orange and yellow.
Cultivation: Grow in full sun or partial shade.
Height: 1m (3ft); *spread:* 45cm (18in).

Trollius europaeus
Native to Europe, this species has deeply divided leaves, 13cm (5in) long, and toothed lobes. The erect stems bear smaller leaves and spherical, lemon-yellow flowers, 5cm (2in) across, in early and midsummer.
Cultivation: Grow in full sun or partial shade.
Height: 60cm (2ft); *spread:* 45cm (18in).

Trollius × *cultorum* cultivar

FERNS

These plants excel in cool, shady places in moist soil near water. Many styles of garden are linked to different types of plant, and the wooded, shady Japanese-type garden makes great use of these subtle plants. Colour is replaced by form, texture and shape, with the fronds offering a huge variation of interest. There are many situations in the Western garden where it would be more sensible to site a pool in shade rather than in the sunniest spot, and a shaded pool surrounded by ferns is the epitome of peace and calm and can be easier to maintain than a pool in full sun.

The following selection includes the most easily grown ferns and those that are most widely available commercially.

Adiantum (Adiantaceae)
Maidenhair fern
The genus contains more than 200 species, which are widely distributed in temperate and tropical areas and which are reasonably adaptable to many soils, although they prefer moist, humus-rich soils with low to medium levels of light.
Propagation: By sowing spores or by division in spring.
Hardiness: Few species are totally hardy unless their rhizomes are covered adequately with a humus-rich mulch in severe winters.

Adiantum aleuticum
Aleutian maidenhair fern, northern maidenhair fern
A deciduous or semi-evergreen species from North America and E. Asia, this fern has short rhizomes which support pale to mid-green, kidney-shaped fronds, 20–30cm (8–12in) long, with numerous segments, black stalks and midribs.
Cultivation: Grow in shade in moist but well-drained soil.
Height and spread: 45cm (18in).

Asplenium
(Aspleniaceae)
Spleenwort
This is a large genus of about 700 widely distributed, mainly tropical and subtropical ferns. Many species produce "bird's nest" type leaf arrangements, and many are epiphytic.
Propagation: By sowing spores or by dividing in early spring.
Hardiness: Hardy to frost tender.

Asplenium scolopendrium (syn. *Phyllitis scolopendrium*, *Scolopendrium vulgare*)
Hart's tongue fern
This is one of the few temperate species native to Europe. It is a hardy terrestrial fern, with irregular shuttle-cock-like crowns of undulating, strap-like, leathery, glossy, bright green fronds, 40cm (16in) or longer, which are heart-shaped at the bases. The ideal planting spot for these plants is the shaded vertical faces of rocky outcrops near waterfalls or streams.
Cultivation: Grow in partial shade in well-drained, rich soil. Avoid full sun.
Height: 45–70cm (18–28in); *spread:* 60cm (2ft).

Athyrium (Woodsiaceae)
The genus includes nearly 200 species of deciduous terrestrial ferns from widely diverse parts of the world, although all prefer moist woodland.
Propagation: By sowing spores as soon as ripe or by dividing in spring.
Hardiness: Hardy to frost tender.

Athyrium filix-femina
Lady fern
This hardy deciduous fern, which is native to Europe, North America and Asia, is one of the most attractive hardy ferns. It has elegant, arching fronds, which are pinnate, lance-shaped and light green. They look like shuttlecocks that splay out towards the edge and each frond grows to 1m (3ft) long.
Cultivation: Grow in moist, neutral to acid soil. It prefers brighter light than most ferns as long as it is filtered.
Height: 1.2m (4ft); *spread:* 60cm–1m (2–3ft).

Adiantum aleuticum

Dryopteris erythrosora

Blechnum (Blechnaceae)
Hard fern
This is a widely distributed genus of about 200 mainly evergreen terrestrial ferns, which are found in sheltered, acid conditions mostly in the southern hemisphere. Some of the tender species develop quite distinctive "trunks".
Propagation: By sowing spores in late summer or by division in spring.
Hardiness: Hardy to frost tender.

Blechnum spicant
Hard fern, deer fern
From northern temperate regions, this hardy evergreen fern makes a strong clump. It produces two types of frond: slender fertile fronds, 30cm–1m (1–3ft) long, which mass together in the centre of the clump, and sterile, deep green, shining fronds that spread flat and are about 45cm (18in) long.
Cultivation: Grow in humus-rich soil in partial or full shade.
Height: 20–50cm (8–20in); *spread:* 60cm (2ft) or more.

Dryopteris
(Dryopteridaceae)
Buckler fern, wood fern
A large genus, containing between 150 and 200 species of terrestrial ferns, these are found mainly in the temperate regions of the northern hemisphere. Mostly deciduous, they will remain almost evergreen in mild winters.
Propagation: By spores as soon as ripe or by dividing older specimens in spring.
Hardiness: Hardy to half hardy.

Asplenium scolopendrium

Matteuccia struthiopteris

Onoclea sensibilis

Osmunda regalis

Dryopteris erythrosora
Japanese shield fern, copper shield fern
Native to Japan and China, this beautiful, frost to half hardy fern produces young fronds, 25–60cm (10–24in) long, of glossy copper and pink, which mature to a rich glossy green. The fronds develop scarlet spore capsules on the undersides.
Cultivation: Grow in shelter and partial shade.
Height: 60cm (2ft); *spread:* 38cm (15in).

Matteuccia (Woodsiaceae)
This a genus of four species of deciduous, terrestrial ferns, common in deciduous woodlands of Europe, east Asia and North America. They are characterized by having two types of frond: the fertile fronds grow erect in the centre while the flatter, sterile ones grow around them. They need moisture all year round.
Propagation: By sowing spores as soon as ripe or by dividing established clumps in spring.
Hardiness: Hardy.

Matteuccia struthiopteris
Ostrich-plume fern, shuttlecock fern
This attractive and graceful hardy fern has lance-shaped, erect, divided fronds, each of which grows to 1.2m (4ft). These are surrounded by shorter, flatter fronds, 30cm (12in) long. Small shuttlecocks can be produced about 10cm (4in) away from the main crown on the spreading rhizomatous roots.
Cultivation: Grow in partial or dappled shade.
Height: 1.7m (5½ft); *spread:* 1m (3ft).

Onoclea (Woodsiaceae)
The genus contains a single species of deciduous hardy, terrestrial ferns from temperate regions of east Asia and North America.
Propagation: By sowing the spores as soon as they are ripe or by dividing established clumps in spring.
Hardiness: Hardy.

Onoclea sensibilis
Sensitive fern
This fern can quickly clothe large areas of moist soil with dense carpets of arching, divided, triangular or lance-shaped fronds, each to about 60cm (2ft) long. The fronds may be pinkish bronze in the spring.
Cultivation: Grow in light dappled shade; the fronds will burn if they are exposed to strong midday sun.
Height: 60cm (2ft); *spread:* indefinite.

Osmunda (Osmundaceae)
Flowering fern
The genus includes 12 species of hardy, deciduous, terrestrial ferns which are found everywhere except Australasia.
Propagation: By spores sown as soon as ripe or by dividing established clumps in spring or autumn.
Hardiness: Hardy.

Polystichum setiferum Divisilobum Group

Osmunda regalis
Royal fern
One of the finest ferns for the waterside, this species has sterile fronds, to 1.2–1.5m (4–5ft) long, which are a delicate pale green tinted with coppery brown when young. They are particularly beautiful when they unfurl and provide a double bonus in the autumn when they develop a deep russet colour before the frosts. Erect pale brown fertile fronds are very conspicuous in the centre of the clump.
Cultivation: Grow in partial shade and cover the rootstock in the winter with a humus-rich mulch.
Height: 1.8 (6ft); *spread:* 4m (13ft).

Polypodium (Polypodiaceae)
This is a large genus of about 75 cosmopolitan ferns, most of which are evergreen, with leathery fronds and rhizomes close to ground level. These ferns are suitable for the sides of streams where the humidity is high but the surface roots are not waterlogged.
Propagation: By sowing spores when ripe or by division in spring.
Hardiness: Hardy to frost tender.

Polypodium vulgare

Polypodium vulgare
Common polpody
A hardy evergreen fern, from temperate regions, this species is a colonizer of damp places where there is adequate drainage. If left undisturbed, it will form large clumps of long, deep green, deeply cut fronds, 8cm (3in) wide, which look particularly fine in a wild garden. The surface rhizomes are thickly matted with hairy brown scales.
Cultivation: Grow in sun or dappled shade with shelter from wind.
Height: 30cm (1ft); *spread:* indefinite.

Polystichum (Dryopteridaceae)
The genus contains nearly 200 species of terrestrial ferns, usually remaining evergreen, from a wide cosmopolitan distribution. They enjoy moist, well-shaded and well-drained conditions.
Propagation: By sowing spores when ripe or by division in spring.
Hardiness: Hardy to frost tender.

Polystichum setiferum
Soft shield fern, hedge fern, English hedge fern
Native to Europe, this is one of the most tolerant of the hardy evergreen ferns, surviving in sun or shade and in moist or dry soil. When grown in moist, shady spots it assumes its true elegance, with softly textured, dull green, lance-shaped, pinnate fronds, 30cm–1.2m (1–4ft) long. The stems are partly encased in soft brown scales, which creep up the frond. The fronds of *P. setiferum* Divisilobum Group are covered in white scales.
Cultivation: Grow in partial shade.
Height: 1.2m (4ft); *spread:* 1m (3ft).

ORNAMENTAL GRASSES

With the immediate margins of a pond being dominated by the grass-like foliage of reeds, rushes and sedges, the foliage of true grasses makes a natural transition to the drier soils away from the pool possible. Although some of the ornamental grasses prefer a drier soil, there are several species that need ample moisture to attain their full stature and flower potential. Although they are easy to grow, requiring no more than cutting down hard each spring, they have been a much neglected group of plants for the water garden, but with the advent of a more natural approach to planting schemes they are becoming increasingly popular again. There are grasses for every situation in the garden, including stream sides and rocky banks. Some have such impressive, tall flowers that it is difficult to resist planting them where their reflections can be seen in the water.

The following selection includes some of the main genera that prefer slightly moister conditions.

Calamagrostis (Poaceae)
Reed grass
This genus contains about 250 species of perennial, tufted grasses, tolerant of all but the poorest of soil conditions.
Propagation: By division in spring.
Hardiness: Hardy.

Calamagrostis × *acutiflora* 'Stricta'
Feather reed grass
Its elegant inflorescence, architectural form and long-lasting character make this an extremely useful grass. It is an erect, clump-forming plant, which has slightly glossy, narrow, dark green leaves and shiny, green, straight stems. The stems bear slender panicles, which open to reveal subtle purple tints. After flowering the heads close up and become slender again, changing colour to a deep beige. The heads are held throughout winter. *C.* × *acutiflora* 'Overdam' is smaller at 1.2m (4ft), with leaves with pale yellow margins and stripes which fade with age, while the purple flower-heads become greyish pink as the summer advances.
Cultivation: Grow in full sun or partial shade.
Height: 1.5m (5ft); *spread:* 60cm–1.2m (2–4ft).

Carex oshimensis 'Evergold'

Carex (Cyperaceae)
Sedge
This genus contains about 1,000 species, which are distributed throughout the world in temperate and tropical areas. Sedges are very versatile and can be used in nearly every part of the garden. Some species are also described in the section on marginal plants, but the one that is described here prefers much more oxygen around its roots than many of the other sedges.
Propagation: By division.
Hardiness: Hardy to frost tender.

Deschampsia cespitosa

Carex oshimensis 'Evergold' (syn. *C.* 'Evergold')
This hardy clump-forming cultivar provides a splash of colour for the pond margins where there is good drainage. It produces fountain-like tussocks of dark green leaves, each with a wide, creamy-yellow central stripe. The brown flower spikes are borne on stems 15cm (6in) long in mid- and late spring.
Cultivation: Grow in full sun or partial shade.
Height: 30cm (12in); *spread:* 35cm (14in).

Deschampsia (Poaceae)
Hair grass
There are about 50 species of hardy, tufted grasses in the genus. They are found in the cooler parts of the northern hemisphere, and they look exceptionally attractive when they are grouped beside water where the light, airy and wispy panicles are caught by the sun.
Propagation: By division in spring.
Hardiness: Hardy.

Deschampsia cespitosa
Tufted hair grass
This delicate ornamental grass forms dense tufts of narrow, rough-edged, arching, dark green leaves, which send up numerous, erect, slender stems, from which hang

Hakonechloa macra 'Alboaurea'

dainty, open panicles of tiny, greenish-purple flowers. These have the added advantage of turning to brownish-yellow spikelets that last into the winter.
Cultivation: Grow in full sun or partial shade.
Height: 1m (3ft); *spread:* 60cm (2ft).

Hakonechloa (Poaceae)
The genus contains a single species of deciduous, clump-forming, perennial mountain grasses. The species, *H. macra*, is native to Japan, where it prefers the cool shade of woodland margins and moist, but well-drained soil.
Propagation: By division in spring.
Hardiness: Hardy.

Hakonechloa macra 'Alboaurea'
This hardy grass makes a lovely specimen or group plant in Japanese-style water gardens, where it forms a rounded cushion of tapering foliage. The leaves are variegated with yellow and green stripes, and turn russet in the autumn. Small flowers are borne in summer and early autumn. It thrives in moisture-retentive soil and is suitable for growing in a container.
Cultivation: Grow in partial shade for the best variegation.
Height and spread: To 45cm (18in).

Calamagrostis × *acutiflora* 'Overdam'

Miscanthus (Poaceae)

There are between 17 and 20 species in the genus of perennial grasses, which occur from Africa to Asia in moist meadows and marshland. The leaves are reed-like but the full beauty lies in the flower-heads of spikelets above the leaves in late summer.
Propagation: By division.
Hardiness: Hardy to frost hardy.

Miscanthus sinensis

Native to Japan and China, this hardy vigorous clump-forming grass has flat, long, blue-green leaves, to 1.2m (4ft) long. The autumn flowers form pyramidal spikes about 40cm (16in) long of silky, hairy, pale grey spikelets tinted maroon or purple-brown.
Cultivation: Grow in well-drained soil in full sun.
Height: 4m (13ft); *spread:* 1.2m (4ft).

Miscanthus sinensis 'Kleine Fontäne'

This hardy cultivar has a narrow, vertical habit of green leaves and thick stems which hold on to the fluffy flower-heads well into the winter.
Cultivation: Grow in full sun.
Height: 1.2m (4ft); *spread:* 60cm (2ft).

Miscanthus sinensis 'Zebrinus'

Zebra grass
This frost hardy cultivar has creamy-white or pale-yellow horizontal banding on arching leaves.
Cultivation: Grow in well-drained soil in full sun.
Height: 1.2m (4ft); *spread:* 1m (3ft).

Molinia (Poaceae)

The genus contains two or three species of densely tufted perennial grasses from Europe and Asia. They have tight or compressed narrow

Miscanthus sinensis 'Kleine Fontäne'

spikes, which sometimes open in autumn to form lovely loose panicles.
Propagation: By division in spring.
Hardiness: Hardy.

Molinia caerulea

Purple moor grass
This grass is a native of European moorlands. It has upright stems topped with tight, purplish flower-heads in late summer which last into the autumn. The foliage is green, with good yellow autumn colour.
Cultivation: Grow in full sun or partial shade and moist soil.
Height: 1.2m (4ft); *spread:* 60cm (2ft).

Panicum (Poaceae)

Crab grass
This widespread genus contains about 470 species of annual, perennial, evergreen and deciduous grasses. They are valued for their light, airy inflorescences, which are panicles with narrow, or more often open, branches.
Propagation: By seed or by division.
Hardiness: Hardy to half hardy.

Pennisetum alopecuroides

Molinia caerulea

Panicum virgatum

Switch grass
This is a narrowly upright, deciduous, hardy perennial with clumps of glaucous, mid-green stems. These bear flat, upright leaves, 60cm (2ft) long, which turn yellow in autumn. The weeping panicles of tiny, purple-green spikelets reach 50cm (20in) in length and appear in autumn.
Cultivation: Grow in full sun.
Height: 1m (3ft); *spread:* 75cm (30in).

Pennisetum (Poaceae)

There are about 80 species of annual and perennial grasses in this genus. They are of mainly tropical origin, but a few species are hardy in temperate regions. They are grown for their feathery, spike-like panicles.
Propagation: By seed or by division in spring or autumn.
Hardiness: Hardy to frost tender.

Pennisetum alopecuroides (syn. *P. compressum*)

Fountain grass
Native to eastern Asia to western Australia, this frost hardy evergreen perennial species produces delightful purple or yellow-green, bottlebrush-like flower spikes, 20cm (8in) long, in autumn. The leaves are deep green, pointed and 30–60cm (1–2ft) long.
Cultivation: Grow in full sun.
Height: 1m (3ft); *spread:* 60cm–1.2m (2–4ft).

Phalaris (Poaceae)

The genus contains about 15 species of temperate perennial and annual grasses from southern Europe and temperate regions of America. They originate from a range of habitats, from dry scrub to moist areas by pools and lakes. They do well in gardens, but can be invasive.

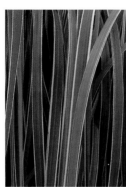

Spartina pectinata 'Aureomarginata'

Panicum virgatum

Propagation: By division in spring or autumn.
Hardiness: Hardy to frost hardy.

Phalaris arundinacea var. picta

Gardener's garters
This erect, hardy perennial grass has flat, narrow, short-pointed, white-striped leaves. In early and midsummer, it bears narrow spikes of pale green flowers, 18cm (7in) long, which fade to buff with age. It is also invasive. 'Feesey' is an improved form of gardener's garters (*P. arundinacea* var. *picta*). It has pink flushes at the base of the stems and light green leaves with broad white stripes. The flower spikes also have a purplish tinge. It is not quite so invasive as the species.
Cultivation: Grow in full sun or partial shade.
Height: 1m (3ft); *spread:* indefinite.

Spartina (Poaceae)

Marsh grass, cord grass
This genus contains about 15 species of tall, perennial grasses, which are native to wet areas of America, Africa and Europe, especially in the subtropical and temperate zones. Only one species is grown in the ornamental water garden, where its flowers associate well with reeds.
Propagation: By division.
Hardiness: Hardy to frost tender.

Spartina pectinata 'Aureomarginata'

This hardy form spreads rapidly by rhizomes. It has strong upright to arching stems, and the leaves have bright yellow variegated margins. The creamy flowers open in mid- to late summer in stiff panicles.
Cultivation: Grow in full sun.
Height: 2.2m (7ft); *spread:* indefinite.

TREES AND SHRUBS

A water garden surrounded purely with herbaceous plants lacks a framework in winter, when both the aquatics and the surrounding plants die back, and brown, dead foliage predominates. The value of the woody growth of trees and shrubs comes into its own at this time of year, when stems, silhouettes and evergreen foliage take on a new dimension when they are reflected in the clear water. Dwarf conifers planted at the side of a watercourse running through rocks complete the setting for a stream at a time when shapes become as important as colour. The following plants are just a few of the trees and shrubs that could be used to create a setting for water. They are tolerant of a wide range of soils and locations.

Abies (Pinaceae)
Silver fir
The genus contains about 50 species of evergreen conifers from Europe, North Africa, Asia and North America. Unlike spruces, which have pendulous cones, those of fir trees are erect. There is a wide range of sizes and shapes, but those described here are ideal for a rocky bank near water.
Propagation: By seed.
Hardiness: Hardy.

Abies cephalonica 'Meyer's Dwarf'
This low, spreading, mounded conifer has short leaves, 9mm–1cm (⅜–½in) long, which are arranged radially around the shoots.
Cultivation: Grow in full sun.
Height: 50cm (20in); *spread:* 1–3m (3–10ft) in time.

Abies koreana 'Silberlocke'
The dimensions indicated are those the tree might be expected to achieve in 10–15 years. This slow-growing, dwarf form of the Korean fir has needlelike leaves, which tend to twist above the fawn-coloured shoots revealing the silver undersides. The lateral shoots are effective when hanging over a small stream.
Cultivation: Grow in full sun.
Height: 1.5–1.8m (5–6ft); *spread:* 1.2m (4ft).

Abies procera 'Glauca Prostrata'
Although *A. procera* is the stately, noble fir seen in large plantations, this cultivar has a shrubby, rather prostrate habit. Its great attraction is the glaucous bright blue foliage.
Cultivation: Grow in full sun.
Height: 90cm–1.2m (3–4ft) in 10–15 years; *spread:* 1.2–1.5m (4–5ft).

Acer (Aceraceae)
Maple
The large genus contains about 150 species of evergreen and deciduous trees and shrubs from Europe, North Africa, Asia and North and Central America. They vary in size from huge

Abies cephalonica 'Meyer's Dwarf'

trees to small, elegant shrubs, which are incredibly effective when they are reflected in water.
Propagation: By seed.
Hardiness: Hardy to frost tender.

Acer palmatum
Japanese maple
This hardy maple is very familiar in the ornamental garden. It is more likely that one of the cultivars will be grown than the species. The cultivars are much smaller and have interesting variations of the palmate leaves, which turn vivid colours in autumn. *A. palmatum* var. *dissectum*

Acer palmatum var. *dissectum*

has finely cut leaves that turn gold in autumn.
Cultivation: Grow in partial shade. All Japanese maples prefer a moist but well-drained soil and a position that is sheltered from wind.
Height: 7.6m (25ft); *spread:* 10m (30ft).

Acer palmatum f. *atropurpureum*
This impressive and popular Japanese maple has deeply lobed, red-purple leaves, which turn shades of brilliant red in autumn.
Cultivation: Grow in partial shade.
Height: 3m (10ft); *spread:* 4m (13ft).

Alnus incana 'Aurea'

Acer palmatum 'Ōsakazuki'
This is one of the best cultivars for autumn colour. It has large, deeply lobed leaves, 10–13cm (4–5in) long, which turn a brilliant red in autumn.
Cultivation: Grow in partial shade.
Height and spread: 6m (20ft).

Alnus (Betulaceae)
Alder
The genus contains about 35 deciduous trees and shrubs, widely distributed in temperate areas of the northern hemisphere, which tolerate extremely wet soils. Male and female catkins appear on the same tree: the male catkins are cylindrical and 5–15cm (2–6in) long, the female flowers are shorter, woody, and resemble conifer cones.
Propagation: By seed.
Hardiness: Hardy.

Alnus glutinosa
Common alder, European alder, black alder
This hardy species originated in Europe, western Asia and North Africa and is now naturalized in eastern North America. It is a rather slender tree with a central trunk and small, horizontal branches. The broad, dark green, pear-shaped leaves, coarsely toothed and 5–10cm (2–4in) long, are sticky on the upper surface.
Cultivation: Grow in full sun.
Height: 24m (80ft); *spread:* 10m (30ft).

Alnus incana 'Aurea'
This tree is an attractive specimen, with yellow leaves, 10cm (4in) long, which turn pale green in summer, and orange shoots and catkins in winter.
Cultivation: Grow in full sun.
Height: 10m (30ft); *spread:* 4.5m (15ft).

Andromeda (Ericaceae)
The two species in this genus are low-growing, wiry-stemmed evergreen shrubs, found in acid peat bogs in cooler regions of the northern hemisphere. Ideal for a shady streamside.
Propagation: By softwood cuttings in midsummer.
Hardiness: Hardy.

Andromeda polifolia

Betula utilis var. *jacquemontii*

Andromeda polifolia
Bog rosemary
This semi-erect, hardy shrub has pointed, oblong, leathery, dark green leaves, 1–4cm (½–1½in) long. Slender flower stalks carry white or pale pink flowers, 4cm (1½in) across, in spring and early summer.
Cultivation: Grow in full sun or partial shade.
Height: 40cm (16in); *spread:* 60cm (2ft).

Betula (Betulaceae)
Birch
The genus contains about 60 species of deciduous trees which originate from the northern temperate and Arctic regions. They are graceful trees, often with pendulous branches, carrying neat, small leaves and long, swinging catkins in spring. They prefer moist, sandy soil, but many species are adaptable to a variety of soil conditions.
Propagation: By seed.
Hardiness: Hardy.

Betula nigra
River birch, red birch
This North American species forms a graceful pyramidal shape. It is noted for its reddish-brown bark, which takes on a ribboned look as it ages and becomes ragged. The diamond-shaped, glossy, dark green leaves are 8cm (3in) long and turn yellow in autumn.
Cultivation: Grow in full sun.
Height: 15–24m (50–80ft); *spread:* 12m (40ft).

Betula papyrifera
Paper birch
This conical tree has white bark, which peels in thin layers and is pale orange-brown in colour when it is

newly exposed. The oval, dark green leaves grow to 10cm (4in) long and turn yellow to orange in autumn.
Cultivation: Grow in full sun.
Height: 30m (100ft); *spread:* 10m (30ft).

Betula pendula
Siver birch, white birch, common birch
This elegant tree, which is native to Europe and Asia, has silvery, peeling bark that eventually becomes dark and rough at the base. The neat, dainty leaves are 6cm (2½in) long and are carried on pendulous branches.
Cultivation: Grow in full sun.
Height: 18m (60ft); *spread:* to 10m (30ft).

Betula utilis
Himalayan birch
This tree, which is native to China and the Himalayas, has copper-brown or pinkish, peeling bark. The dark green leaves are 13cm (5in) long and turn yellow in autumn. *B. utilis* var. *jacquemontii* has white bark.
Cultivation: Grow in full sun.
Height: 18m (60ft); *spread:* to 10m (30ft).

Cedrus (Pinaceae)
Cedar
The genus contains four species of evergreen coniferous trees, which are native to the Himalayas and Mediterranean littoral. Although they grow to majestic specimen trees, which are too large for the average garden, there are some excellent, small, slow-growing cultivars, which clothe large rock areas and give added interest throughout the year to a watercourse.
Propagation: By seed.
Hardiness: Hardy.

Cedrus deodara 'Feelin' Blue'
The dimensions indicated are those the tree might be expected to achieve in 10–15 years. This is one of the few slow-growing, dwarf cedars with bluish-grey foliage. It hugs the ground and is an excellent specimen at the water's edge.
Cultivation: Grow in well-drained soil in full sun.
Height: 60cm (2ft); *spread:* 1.8m (6ft).

Cedrus deodara 'Golden Horizon'
This is a low-growing cultivar which can be easily kept in check by the judicious removal of leading branches in the spring. It has yellowish or yellowish green foliage when grown in full sun but this becomes a duller blue-green if grown in shade. It is much brighter when grown in full sun.
Cultivation: Grow in well-drained soil.
Height: 1.8m (6ft); *spread:* 3m (10ft).

Chamaecyparis (Cupressaceae)
Cypress, false cypress
The seven or eight species in the genus are evergreen coniferous trees from Taiwan, Japan and North America. They are a common garden conifer, often used for hedging or lawn specimens. There are several dwarf forms available for the sides of rocky watercourses, and the following species is a particularly attractive, slow-growing specimen.
Propagation: By seed.
Hardiness: Hardy.

Chamaecyparis obtusa 'Nana Gracilis'
This attractive conifer will take many years to reach the dimensions noted below. It has a very dense, pyramidal habit with rich green foliage, which has a slightly curly appearance.
Cultivation: Grow in full sun.
Height: 3m (10ft); *spread:* 1.2m (4ft).

Cornus (Cornaceae)
Dogwood, cornel
The genus contains about 45 species of mainly deciduous trees and shrubs, distributed widely over temperate parts of the northern hemisphere. Many of the shrubs thrive in wet situations, where their coloured stems are reflected in the water. The species grown for their stem colour should be cut back hard in spring to encourage the strong growth of the new stems.
Propagation: By seed or by hardwood cuttings.
Hardiness: Hardy to frost hardy.

Cornus alba
Red-barked dogwood
This hardy, rampant, deciduous species from Siberia and northern China has stems that become blood-red in winter. It bears oval, dark green leaves, 10cm (4in) long, which turn red or orange in autumn. White flowers are borne in flat cymes, about 5cm (2in) across, in late spring and early summer, and develop into white, blue-tinged oval fruit. 'Spaethii' is a superb form with the most attractive variegated leaves, which are green with yellow margins.
Cultivation: Grow in full sun.
Height and spread: 3m (10ft).

Chamaecyparis obtusa 'Nana Gracilis'

Cornus mas

Cornus mas
Cornelian cherry
This hardy deciduous species from
Europe and west Asia has dark green
leaves, 10cm (4in) long, which turn
purplish red in autumn. In later
winter, before the leaves appear,
yellow flowers are produced in
umbels, up to 2cm (¾in) across.
Bright red, edible fruits are produced
in late summer.
Cultivation: Grow in full sun.
Height and spread: 4.5m (15ft).

Cornus sanguinea 'Winter Beauty'
This hardy cultivar is not as
vigorous as many of the *C. alba* and
C. sanguinea cultivars, but has bright
orange and yellow winter shoots.
Cultivation: Grow in full sun.
Height: 3m (10ft); *spread:* 2.4m (8ft).

Cornus stolonifera
Red osier dogwood
This hardy species has dark-red stems
in winter. It is a vigorous, suckering
shrub, with oval, dark green leaves,
about 13cm (5in) long, which turn
red or orange in autumn. The white
flowers are borne in flat cymes, 5cm
(2in) across, in late spring and early
summer and are followed by white
fruit, often tinged blue.
Cultivation: Grow in full sun or
partial shade.
Height: 1.8m (6ft); *spread:* 4m (13ft).

Cornus stolonifera 'Flaviramea'
This hardy dogwood has yellow
stems, which need regular pruning to
encourage the coloration in the
shoots. If left unpruned, terminal
clusters of whitish-cream berries are
produced in autumn.

Metasequoia glyptostroboides

Cultivation: Grow in full sun or
partial shade.
Height: 1.2m (4ft); *spread:* 4m (13ft).

Metasequoia
(Taxodiaceae)
The genus contains a single species of
deciduous conifer, discovered in the
1940s in China. Tolerant of waterlogged soils, it quickly becomes
established as a narrow specimen tree.
Propagation: By seed.
Hardiness: Hardy.

Metasequoia glyptostroboides
Dawn redwood, water larch
This is a moisture-loving, fast-growing
tree with an attractive, reddish, fibrous
bark, which becomes fluted with age.
Growing in a narrow conical habit, it
briefly assumes attractive autumn
colours when its small larch-like, soft
green leaves, about 1cm (½in) long,
turn yellow and orange before falling.
Cultivation: Grow in full sun.
Height: 30–35m (100–115ft); *spread:*
4.5m (15ft).

Picea (Pinaceae)
Spruce
The genus includes 30–40 species of
coniferous, evergreen trees, occurring
in cool temperate regions of the
northern hemisphere. Many are
grown for timber, but there are some
excellent specimen trees, which look
lovely used as a background to a large
pool and planted to be reflected in
the water. There are also a number of
small cultivars, which are suitable for
planting on rock banks by streams.
Propagation: By seed.
Hardiness: Hardy to frost hardy. (Those
described here are hardy.)

Picea breweriana
Brewer's spruce
This is a slow-growing, columnar tree
with level branches and pendulous
side branches. Blunt-ended flat leaves
are deep green above and whitish
beneath, 2.5–4cm (1–1½in) long, and
there are pendulous cones, 8–14cm
(3–5½in) long. The drooping tips to
the shoots make this a most elegant
specimen tree.
Cultivation: Grow in full sun.
Height: 10–15m (30–50ft); *spread:*
3–4m (10–13ft).

Picea glauca var. albertiana 'Alberta Globe'
This is very similar to *P. albertiana*
'Conica' when small and they are
difficult to tell apart. As it matures, it
develops a more flattened, globose,
bush shape, rather than the more
typical cone shape.
Cultivation: Grow in full sun.
Height: 1.5m (5ft); *spread:* 1m (3ft).

Picea glauca var. albertiana 'Conica'
This garden gem is a neat, cone-
shaped conifer growing to a dwarf
bushy shape. It is a first-class rockery
plant, reaching 75 by 30cm (30 by
12in) in ten years, but which can be
kept tight by annual trimming.
Cultivation: Grow in full sun.
Height: 1.8–6m (6–20ft); *spread:*
1–2.4m (3–8ft).

Pinus (Pinaceae)
Pine
The large genus contains about 120
species of evergreen conifers, which
are widely distributed in the northern
hemisphere. Pines are versatile
plants, being used in forestry and as
windbreaks and specimen trees, while
some dwarf species make a strong
impact in a rock garden. They are

distinguished by having needlelike
leaves, which are clasped at the base
in twos, threes or fives.
Propagation: By seed.
Hardiness: Hardy to frost hardy.
(Those described here are hardy.)

Pinus mugo
Dwarf mountain pine
A spreading, almost shrubby pine,
this has well-spaced pairs of dark to
mid-green leaves, 3–8cm (1¼–3in)
long. It looks good among rocks.
Cultivation: Grow in full sun.
Height: 3.4m (11ft); *spread:* 4.5m
(15ft).

Pinus mugo 'Corley's Mat'
The mountain pine has produced
several seedlings of which this cultivar
is one of the better forms. It has a
tighter habit than the species, forming
a compact, rounded bun of short
needles suitable for rock gardens.
Cultivation: Grow in full sun.
Height: Up to 60cm (2ft); *spread:* to
1.2m (4ft).

Pinus sylvestris 'Watereri'
This dwarf form of the common
Scots pine is a dense specimen, with
an upright habit and needles, 5–8cm
(2–3in) long, held in pairs.
Cultivation: Grow in full sun.
Height: 4m (13ft); *spread:* 7m (23ft).

Salix (Salicaceae)
The genus contains around 300
species of trees and shrubs from the
cooler parts of the temperate
northern hemisphere. Several species
thrive in wet or moist soil, and can be
used as specimen plants or as group
plantings for winter bark colour.
Propagation: By softwood cuttings in
summer or hardwood cuttings
in autumn.
Hardiness: Hardy.

Picea glauca albertiana 'Alberta Globe'

Pinus mugo 'Corley's Mat'

Salix alba 'Chermesina'

Salix integra 'Hakuro-nishiki'

Salix alba 'Chermesina'
Scarlet willow
This cultivar of the more common *S. alba* (white willow) provides a blaze of colour in winter with its brilliant display of scarlet-orange branches. It is particularly effective when prevented from growing into a tree and pruned hard each spring to ensure there is a regular supply of young bushy branches near the ground.
Cultivation: Grow in full sun.
Height: 18–24m (60–80ft); *spread:* 10m (30ft).

Salix alba var. sericea (syn. *S. alba* f. *argentea*)
Silver willow
The common name derives from the silvery grey leaves. This is a smaller, less vigorous form than *S. alba*.
Cultivation: Grow in full sun.
Height: 15m (50ft); *spread:* 8m (26ft).

Salix alba subsp. *vitellina* 'Britzensis'
This cultivar is grown more for its orange-red bark than as a tree. It is very similar to the cultivar *S. alba* 'Chermesina', under which name it is sometimes sold. It is best cut hard back each spring rather than allowed to grow into a full-sized tree.
Cultivation: Grow in full sun.
Height: 18m (60ft); *spread:* 8m (26ft).

Salix babylonica var. pekinensis 'Tortuosa' (syn. *S. matsudana* 'Tortuosa')
Corkscrew willow, contorted willow
This is a cultivar of a species that is native to northern China and Korea. It is one of the most striking and easily identified of the willows because of the remarkable corkscrew

arrangement of the branches and leaves, which are also twisted.
Cultivation: Grow in full sun.
Height: 12–15m (40–50ft); *spread:* 8m (26ft).

Salix caprea
Goat willow, pussy willow
This common, spreading, deciduous tree from Europe and Asia has golden catkins, which appear in spring. The broad leaves are oblong and downy at first, woolly beneath and grey-green in colour. This tree is suitable only for large-scale planting in natural areas, but for garden use there is a grafted weeping tree called *S. caprea* 'Kilmarnock', which grows to 1.5–1.8m (5–6ft) high and is much better suited to waterside planting.
Cultivation: Grow in full sun.
Height: 6–10m (20–30ft); *spread:* 6m (20ft).

Salix daphnoides
Violet willow
This tree, which is native to Europe, bears shoots that are downy at first, then become purple with a waxy bloom. The leaves are oval to lance shaped, smooth and shiny, 12cm (5in) long. This is ideal for a wildlife pond.
Cultivation: Grow in full sun.
Height: 10–12m (30–40ft); *spread:* to 6m (20ft).

Salix exigua
Coyote willow
Native to North America, this upright, thicket-forming, suckering shrub has narrow, grey-green leaves, which grow to about 10cm (4in) in length, and will do well on sandy soils.
Cultivation: Grow in full sun.
Height: 4m (13ft); *spread:* 4.5m (15ft).

Salix gracilistyla 'Melanostachys'
A spreading, bushy shrub, this has arching shoots, which are silky and hairy when young, and finely toothed and grey-green when mature. It has the most distinctive catkins, which are black with brick-red anthers.
Cultivation: Grow in full sun.
Height: 3m (10ft); *spread:* 4m (13ft).

Salix integra 'Hakuro-nishiki'
This willow is actually a shrub, which is usually sold grafted onto a clear stem to create a round-headed, miniature tree. The leaves, variegated with pink and cream, keep a good colour well into summer.
Cultivation: Grow in full sun.
Height: 1.5m (5ft); *spread:* 1m (3ft).

Salix lanata
Woolly willow
This shrubby species is native to northern Europe. The buds and young branches are covered with soft, grey hairs. It looks beautiful when it is allowed to form grey mounds at the waterside.
Cultivation: Grow in full sun.
Height: 90cm (3ft); *spread:* to 1.5m (5ft).

Taxodium (Taxodiaceae)
Bald cypress
The three species in this genus are ornamental, pyramid-shaped, deciduous conifers, which are native to the southeastern United States and Mexico. They are semi-aquatic in their native habitat but are also capable of thriving in ordinary soils. They are generally too large for the small to average-size garden.
Propagation: By seed.
Hardiness: Hardy.

Taxodium distichum
Swamp cypress
This species has a narrow pyramidal habit. The soft, deciduous, flat leaves are short, only 2.5cm (1in) long, yellowish-green in colour and turn brown in autumn in two ranks. Buttressed roots, known as "knees", can appear in shallow water. For garden use it has been largely superseded by the smaller *Metasequoia glyptostroboides* (dawn redwood).
Cultivation: Grow in full sun.
Height: 30–37m (100–120ft); *spread:* 6–8.5m (20–28ft).

Vaccinium (Ericaceae)
Bilberry, blueberry, cranberry
There are about 450 species of deciduous and evergreen shrubs and some small trees in this genus. Some species are grown for their edible fruits, and the more ornamental species are ideal for an acid soil along a shady waterside.
Propagation: By seed or by softwood cuttings.
Hardiness: Hardy to frost hardy.

Vaccinium macrocarpon
Cranberry
This is a hardy, prostrate, mat-forming evergreen shrub. The oblong leaves are shiny, dark green, 2.5cm (1in) long, and turn bronze in the winter. Bell-shaped, pink flowers, 1cm (½in) across, are produced singly in the summer and are followed by edible, spherical, red berries.
Cultivation: Grow in sun or partial shade.
Height: 15cm (6in); *spread:* indefinite.

Taxodium distichum

ALPINES

To complete the range of plants required to make a water garden with an associated rock feature, this section includes some scrambling plants that can be grown in dry soil along the edges of streams, rock pools and small pools that have been made with preformed units. The soil at the sides of these features can be dry, particularly if the feature is built into a mound of soil. Despite the normal association with moisture-loving plants along these edges, these would not do well if planted in a dry soil, and it is far better to use alpines that are capable of thriving in these conditions.

Antennaria (Asteraceae)
Cat's ears
The genus contains about 45 species of evergreen and semi-evergreen, mat-forming perennials, widely distributed in the northern hemisphere. These accommodating ground-cover plants are excellent for crevices or between paving.
Propagation: By seed.
Hardiness: Hardy.

Antennaria dioica
This useful carpeting plant has tufts of grey leaves. The leaves are covered with white hairs on the underside. In summer small fluffy, rose-pink flowers are produced.
Cultivation: Grow in full sun.
Height: 5cm (2in); *spread:* 45cm (18in).

Arenaria
(Caryophyllaceae)
Sandwort
This is a genus of about 160 species of annuals and low-growing perennials, some of which are evergreen, from northern regions of the northern hemisphere. They hug the ground and make excellent plants for screes and rock crevices, where they soon spread over the rock faces.
Propagation: By seed.
Hardiness: Hardy.

Arenaria balearica
Corsican sandwort
A useful, small, prostrate, evergreen, mat-forming perennial, this has minute, shiny, light green leaves. These green carpets break into a sheet of clear white, star-like flowers in late spring.
Cultivation: Grow in partial shade.
Height: 1cm (½in); *spread:* 30cm (1ft).

Aurinia (Brassicaceae)
This genus comprises seven species of clump-forming biennials or evergreens from Europe, Russia and Turkey, where they grow in rocky, mountainous areas. They are robust growing plants, frequently used to clothe dry walls and large rock banks.
Propagation: By seed or by softwood cuttings.
Hardiness: Hardy.

Aurinia saxatilis (syn. *Alyssum saxatile*)
Gold dust
This is a reliable, mound-forming, evergreen perennial. The grey-green, hairy, toothed leaves grow in rosettes, and in late spring and early summer the plants are covered with bright yellow, four-petalled flowers.
Cultivation: Grow in full sun.
Height: 20cm (8in); *spread:* 30cm (12in).

Campanula
(Campanulaceae)
The large genus contains 300 annuals, biennials and perennials, distributed widely throughout temperate regions of the northern hemisphere, in habitats ranging from meadows and woodland to rocky slopes. Many species are suitable for rock and scree gardens and form cushions of spreading, tight, green leaves.
Propagation: By seed or softwood cuttings.
Hardiness: Hardy to frost tender. (Those described here are hardy.)

Campanula carpatica
This widely grown herbaceous bellflower from the Carpathian mountains forms small tufts with bright green, oval, sharply toothed leaves. The upright, bell-shaped flowers, 2.5–4cm (1–1½in) across, are violet, purple, blue or white and appear in summer and autumn.
Cultivation: Grow in sun or partial shade. They are at their best in well-drained soil.
Height and spread: 20–30cm (8–12in).

Campanula portenshlagiana (syn. *C. muralis*)
Dalmatian bellflower
This is an old favourite in the garden. It is a perennial, semi-trailing evergreen, which has kidney-shaped, glossy, mid-green leaves. In midsummer sumptuous, tubular to funnel-shaped, violet to deep purple flowers are borne in profusion.
Cultivation: Grow in sun or partial shade. They are at their best in well-drained soil.
Height: 15cm (6in); *spread:* 50cm (20in).

Campanula poscharskyana
This vigorous, trailing perennial spreads by underground runners. It is a good selection for bolder parts of a rock garden, producing a glorious tangle of long, slender branches which bear downy, mid-green leaves. From midsummer to autumn, constellations of pretty, star-shaped, pale lavender flowers appear.

Campanula portenschlagiana

Cultivation: Grow in sun or partial shade.
Height: 15cm (6in); *spread:* 60cm (2ft).

Cerastium
(Caryophyllaceae)
The genus of about 100 species of annuals and carpet-forming tufted perennials is widely distributed in temperate zones of Europe and North America. The species recommended here is very vigorous and a classic spreader for the most difficult situations where it seldom fails.
Propagation: By seed or by softwood cuttings.
Hardiness: Hardy.

Cerastium tomentosum
Snow-in-summer
This is a rampant, seemingly indestructible, mat-forming perennial, which will give the most astonishing display of gleaming white blooms under the most adverse conditions. There are woolly, silvery-white leaves, and in late spring and summer a profusion of star-like white flowers appears.
Cultivation: Grow in full sun in any soil.
Height: 5–8cm (2–3in); *spread:* indefinite.

Antennaria dioica

Campanula carpatica

Convolvulus
(Convolvulaceae)
This is a large genus containing 250 species of climbing and scrambling annuals and perennials and some evergreen sub-shrubs and perennials. They originate from a diverse range of habitats in subtropical and temperate areas. The scrambling and bushy forms make good, quick covering plants for the hard edges of preformed units.
Propagation: By division in spring.
Hardiness: Hardy to half hardy.

Convolvulus sabatius
(syn. *C. mauritanicus*)
This is a slender-stemmed, trailing, half hardy perennial with mid-green leaves. From summer to early autumn it bears clusters of funnel-shaped, pale to deep lavender-blue flowers.
Cultivation: Grow in full sun. It loves a gritty well-drained soil on a bank.
Height: 15cm (6in); *spread:* 50cm (20in).

Diascia (Scrophulariaceae)
There are 50 species of annuals and semi-evergreen, suckering perennials in the genus, which are found in mountain regions of southern Africa. They have become popular for their long flowering season, when mainly pinkish-red flowers are produced on bushy plants, which quickly cover difficult areas.
Propagation: By seed or by softwood cuttings.
Hardiness: Borderline hardy.

Diascia rigescens
This is an excellent plant for well-drained soils, where it will give a profusion of flowers the whole summer long. It is a trailing perennial with stiff, branching stems and mainly stalkless, toothed, heart-shaped leaves. The mid- to deep salmon-pink flowers, with short, incurved spurs, are produced on tall dense spikes.
D. rigescens 'Variegata' is an attractive cultivar with creamy, variegated leaves.
Cultivation: Grow in full sun. Dead-head to extend the flowering season.
Height: 20cm (8in); *spread:* 50cm (20in).

Erigeron (Asteraceae)
Fleabane
This genus of about 200 species of annuals, biennials and perennials has a wide distribution, especially in North America where the plants are found in dry grassland and mountainous areas. They have become popular in coastal gardens on sandy soil for their ability to resist drought.
Propagation: By seed or by division in spring.
Hardiness: Hardy.

Erigeron karvinskianus
(syn. *E. mucronatus*)
An easily grown little charmer, this species is very suitable for crevices in walls and paving. Carpeting and with a rhizomatous root, this vigorous spreading perennial has grey-green, hairy leaves on lax, branching stems. In summer masses of yellow-centred, daisy-like flower-heads are produced, opening white and gradually fading through pink and purple.
Cultivation: Grow in full or partial shade in well-drained soil.
Height: 15–30cm (6–12in); *spread:* 1m (3ft).

Cerastium tomentosum

Convolvulus sabatius

Geranium (Geraniaceae)
Cranesbill
There are about 300 species of annuals, biennials and herbaceous perennials in the genus, widely distributed in all temperate regions except very damp habitats. They should not be confused with pelargoniums, whose common name is geranium. The trailing, mat-forming and spreading species are superb for rock gardens near a stream or as ground cover in partial shade.
Propagation: By seed or by division.
Hardiness: Hardy to half hardy. (Those described here are hardy.)

Geranium cinereum 'Ballerina'
This dwarf evergreen perennial forms rosettes of grey, deeply lobed leaves, 5cm (2in) across. Short-stalked, upward-facing, cup-shaped purplish red flowers, 2.5cm (1in) across, with dark red veins and dark eyes, appear in late spring and early summer.
Cultivation: Grow in full sun.
Height: 15cm (6in); *spread:* 30cm (12in).

Geranium orientalitibeticum
(syn. *G. stapfianum* var. *roseum*)
This is a delightful dwarf perennial with underground, tuberous runners. The marbled dark and pale green leaves are deeply cut with toothed divisions. In summer cup-shaped, pink to deep purplish pink flowers with white centres are produced.
Cultivation: Grow in sun or partial shade.
Height: 30cm (12in); *spread:* 1m (3ft) or more.

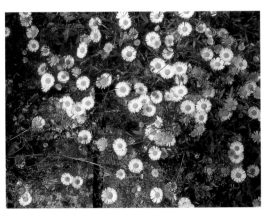

Erigeron karvinskianus

Geranium cinereum 'Ballerina'

Helianthemum
(Cistaceae)
Rock rose, sun rose
The genus contains just over 100
species of evergreen or semi-
evergreen shrubs from North and
South America, Asia, Europe and
North Africa, where they occur in
alpine meadows and open scrub. The
sun or rock roses are an asset to any
garden because they produce flowers
for a very long period in summer.
They are superb in a rock garden
setting, where they can bake in a
well-drained soil and show off their
range of colourful flowers.
Propagation: By seed or by softwood
cuttings.
Hardiness: Hardy to frost hardy.

Helianthemum 'Rhodanthe Carneum'
(syn. *H.* 'Wisley Pink')
This hardy cultivar is a vigorous,
fast-growing, spreading, evergreen
shrub. It has grey leaves and
delicate, saucer-shaped, pale pink
flowers with yellow-orange centres,
which appear in profusion.
Cultivation: Grow in full sun. Cut
back after flowering to keep neat
and dense.
Height: 30cm (12in); *spread:* 45cm
(18in).

Helianthemum 'The Bride'
This hardy cultivar has large white
flowers and grey foliage.
Cultivation: Grow in full sun.
Height: 23cm (9in); *spread:* 25cm
(10in).

Iberis (Brassicaceae)
Candytuft
The genus contains about 40 species
of annuals, perennials and evergreen
sub-shrubs from the Mediterranean
countries, where they are found in
well-drained, open sites. They are an
excellent choice for spreading over
the sides of preformed stream units
and the sides of waterfalls.
Propagation: By seed or by softwood
cuttings.
Hardiness: Hardy to frost tender.

Iberis crenata
From central Spain, this tough, erect
hardy annual has straight, branching
stems and narrow leaves, which are
finely toothed. In spring and early
summer, it produces a dense flower-
head of white flowers that are deeply
notched.
Cultivation: Grow in full sun.
Height and spread: 30cm (12in).

Helianthemum 'Rhodanthe Carneum'

Linum (Linaceae)
A genus of 200 species of evergreen
and deciduous annuals and biennials
from dry, grassy slopes of the
northern hemisphere. They have
colourful funnel to saucer-shaped
flowers and many are suited to
rock gardens where they flower for
long periods.
Propagation: By seed or semi-
ripewood cuttings in summer.
Hardiness: Hardy to frost hardy.

Linum flavum 'Compactum'
This woody, hardy perennial has an
upright habit. The leaves are
spoon-shaped and dark-green,
growing to 2–4cm (¾–1½in) long.
The upward-facing, funnel-shaped,
golden yellow flowers, 2.5cm (1in)
across, appear on the tips of the
many branched stems in summer
when they open in the sunshine.
Cultivation: Do best in full sun on
light, well-drained soils. Protect from
winter wet.
Height and spread: 15cm (6in).

Lithodora
(Boraginaceae)
The seven species in the genus are
low-growing, spreading or erect
evergreen shrubs and sub-shrubs.
They originate from southwestern
Europe to southern Greece, Turkey
and Algeria, where they are found
growing in scrub and thickets.
These plants introduce the loveliest
shade of blue into the rock garden by
the waterside.
Propagation: By semi-ripewood
cuttings.
Hardiness: Hardy to frost hardy.

Helianthemum 'The Bride'

Lithodora diffusa 'Heavenly Blue'
This delightful, prostrate, spreading,
frost hardy evergreen shrub has deep
green, pointed, hairy leaves. In
summer it bears masses of open
funnel-shaped, azure blue flowers.
Cultivation: Grow in full sun in acid,
humus-rich soil.
Height: 15–30cm (6–12in); *spread:*
45cm (18in).

Parahebe
(Scrophulariaceae)
There are 30 species in the genus.
They are evergreen or semi-evergreen
sub-shrubs and perennials, mainly
from Australia and New Zealand,
occurring in dry stony habitats and
screes. Their mat-forming, semi-
prostrate habit makes them suitable
for gravel gardens or rock gardens.

Iberis crenata

Propagation: By seed or by semi-
ripewood cuttings.
Hardiness: Frost hardy.

Parahebe catarractae
This charming, frost hardy evergreen
sub-shrub has oval, sharply toothed,
dark green leaves. The young leaves
are tinged with purple. Sprays of
saucer-shaped white flowers, heavily
shaded and veined with purplish-
pink, are produced in profusion in
the summer.
Cultivation: Grow in full sun.
Height and spread: 30cm (1ft).

Phlox (Polemoniaceae)
A genus of nearly 70 species of
evergreen or herbaceous, low-
growing or mat-forming perennials
mainly found in North America.
The mat and cushion-forming species

Linum flavum 'Compactum'

Pratia pedunculata

Saxifraga cochlearis

Sedum spurium 'Variegatum'

originate in dry, rocky habitats and are therefore suited to growing in rock gardens.
Propagation: By softwood cuttings from non-flowering stems of the cushion-forming types in spring or removing rooted pieces of the trailing forms in early autumn.
Hardiness: Hardy to half hardy.

Phlox subulata
Moss phlox
This dense, evergreen, hardy perennial forms cushions or mats of narrow, bright green leaves, 5mm–2cm (¼–¾in) long. The flowers can be purple, red, lilac, pink or white, 1–2.5cm (½–1in) across, appearing in a star-like formation of petals in spring and early summer.
Cultivation: Grow in full sun.
Height: 5–15cm (2–6in); *spread:* to 50cm (20in).

Phlox subulata 'Emerald Cushion Blue'
This hardy cultivar of the moss phlox has lilac flowers and hugs the ground in dense mats.
Cultivation: Grow in full sun.
Height: No higher than 5cm (2in); *spread:* to 60cm (24in).

Pratia (Campanulaceae)
The genus contains about 20 species of prostrate, spreading evergreen perennials which originate from Africa, Asia, Australia, New Zealand and South America, where they are found growing in damp, shady habitats. They are superb plants for growing in the crevices between rocks with a shady aspect or for forming deep green "grouting" between paving stones, and they like the dampness produced by a nearby watercourse or pool.
Propagation: By division.
Hardiness: Hardy to frost hardy.

Pratia pedunculata
A ground cover for moist conditions, this vigorous, invasive, ground-hugging, hardy perennial has small, rounded leaves and is covered with star-shaped, pale to mid-blue flowers over a long period in summer.
Cultivation: Grow in partial or deep shade.
Height: 1cm (½in); *spread:* indefinite.

Saxifraga (Saxifragaceae)
This is a large genus of more than 400 species of mat or cushion-forming, evergreen or deciduous perennials from a wide distribution in the northern hemisphere, where they are found in mountainous regions. They have a wide variation in habit and leaf form and are widely grown in rock gardens, where they appreciate well-drained soil.
Propagation: By seed or by separating offsets from parent rosettes.
Hardiness: Hardy.

Saxifraga cochlearis
This plant forms a dense cushion of spoon-shaped, mid-green leaves, 4cm (1½in) long, with lime-encrusted margins. In early summer, flower-heads, 6–10cm (2½–4in) long, of white flowers, sometimes red-spotted, rise above a cushion of dense rosettes.
Cultivation: Grow in full sun.
Height: 20cm (8in); *spread:* 15cm (6in).

Saxifraga 'Tumbling Waters'
This is a slow-growing, mat-forming evergreen perennial. It grows in tight rosettes of narrow, lime-encrusted, silvery leaves. When mature, after several years, dense, arching conical heads of small, open cup-shaped, white flowers are produced, after which the main rosette dies and the small offsets grow on.
Cultivation: Grow in full sun.
Height: 60cm (2ft); *spread:* 20–30cm (8–12in).

Sedum (Crassulaceae)
Stonecrop
This large genus contains around 400 species. It is a diverse group of plants, many of which are succulent. They originate from the northern hemisphere, where they are found growing in mountainous and arid regions. These are ideal plants for withstanding difficult conditions such as drought and strong sunshine, and some of the alpine types have a creeping, scrambling habit, which will cover rock edges.
Propagation: By seed or by softwood cuttings.
Hardiness: Hardy to frost tender.

Sedum acre
Common stonecrop, biting stonecrop
This evergreen, mat-forming, hardy perennial has dense, spreading shoots covered in minute, fleshy, triangular, pale green leaves and flat-topped heads of tiny, star-shaped yellow-green flowers.
Cultivation: Grow in full sun.
Height: 5cm (2in); *spread:* 60cm (2ft) or more.

Sedum spathulifolium
This mat-forming, hardy perennial has rosettes of spoon-shaped, fleshy, brittle green or silver leaves, often tinted with bronze and purple. Sprays of tiny, star-shaped, bright yellow flowers appear in summer.
Cultivation: Grow in full sun or light shade.
Height: 5cm (2in); *spread:* indefinite.

Sedum spurium 'Variegatum'
This vigorous, mat-forming, frost hardy evergreen perennial has branching red stems and variegated leaves, 2.5cm (1in) long. Star-shaped, pink, purple or white flowers, 2cm (¾in) across, are produced in rounded flowerheads, 4cm (1.5in) across in late summer.
Cultivation: Grow in full sun.
Height: 10cm (4in); *spread:* to 60cm (2ft).

Veronica (Scrophulariaceae)
Speedwell, brooklime
This genus contains about 250 species, growing in diverse habitats, mainly in Europe. Some are cushion- or mat-forming species and can be used to soften unsightly edges.
Propagation: By seed or by division in autumn.
Hardiness: Hardy to frost hardy.

Veronica prostrata
Prostrate speedwell
This mat-forming, hardy species has bright to mid-green, oval and toothed leaves. In early summer, it produces erect spikes of small, saucer-shaped flowers of a most brilliant blue.
Cultivation: Grow in fairly poor, well-drained soil in full sun.
Height: 15cm (6in); *spread:* 40cm (16in).

Veronica prostrata

SUPPLIERS

UNITED KINGDOM

General distributors of a wide range of water garden products

Blagden Water Gardens
Bath Road
Upper Langford
North Somerset BS18 7DN
Tel: 01934 853531

Bradshaws
Nicolson Link
Clifton Moor
York YO1 1SS
Tel: 01904 691169

Heissner UK Ltd.
Regency Business Centre
Queens Road
Kenilworth
Warwickshire CV8 1JQ
Tel: 01926 851166
Fax: 01926 851151
email: heissner@regency
businesscentre.co.uk
Hozelock Cyprio Ltd.
Waterslade House

Haddenham
Aylesbury
Buckinghamshire HP17 8JD
Tel: 01844 291881

Lotus Water Garden Products
P.O. Box 36
Junction Street
Burnley
Lancashire BB12 ONA
Tel: 01282 420771

Oase (UK) Ltd.
3 Telford Gate
Whittle Road
West Portway Industrial Estate
Andover
Hampshire SP10 3SF
Tel: 01264 333225

Stapeley Water Gardens Ltd.
London Road
Stapeley
Nantwich
Cheshire
CW5 7LH
Tel: 01270 623868

Trident Water Garden Products
Carlton Road
Folehill
Coventry CV6 7FL
Tel: 024 7663 8802

Specialist Suppliers

Civil Engineering Developments Ltd.
728 London Road
West Thurrock
Grays
Essex RM16 1LU
Tel: 01708 867237
Rock supplier
Interpret
Interpret House

Vincent Lane
Dorking
Surrey RH4 3YX
Tel: 01306 881033
Fish foods and medicines

Pinks Hill Landscape Merchants
Broad Street
Wood Street Village
Guildford
Surrey
Tel: 01483 571620
Rock supplier

Rein Ltd.
Clifton Hall
Ashbourne
Derbyshire DE6 2GL
Tel: 01335 342265
Reinforced fibres for mortar

Tetra
Lambert Court
Chestnut Avenue
Eastleigh
Hampshire SO53 3ZQ
Tel: 023 8064 3339
Fish foods and medicines

Volclay Limited
Leonard House
Scotts Quay
Birkenhead
Merseyside L41 1FB
Tel: 0151 638 0967
Clay liners

Wychwood Waterlily and Carp Farm
Farnham Road
Odiham
Hook
Hampshire RG29 1HS
Tel: 0256 702800
Fish supplier

UNITED STATES

General distributors of a wide range of water garden products

Hyannis Country Garden
380 West Main Street
Hyannis, MA 02601
www.gardengoods.com

M&S Ponds and Supplies
14053 Midland Road
Poway, CA 92064
Tel: (858) 679-8729
Fax: (858) 679-5804

North American Rock Garden Society
P.O. Box 67
Millwood, NY 10546
www.hubris.net/nargs.org

Speciality Suppliers

Garden Rock Covers
P.O. Box 1133
Friday Harbor, WA98250
www.gardenrockcovers.com

Select Stone Inc.
P.O. Box 6403
Bozeman, MT 59771
Tel: (406) 582-1000
Fax: (406) 582-1069
www.selectstone.com

Sticks and Stones Farm
197 Huntingtown Road
Newtown, CT 06470
www.sticksandstonesfarm.com

CANADA

Aquascape Ontario
9295 Colborne Street Ext
Chatham
ON N7M 5J4
Tel: (888) 547-POND
Fax: (519) 352-1357
Aquatics & Co.
Box 445

Pickering, ON N7M 5J4
Tel: (905) 668-5326
Fax: (905) 668-4518
www.aquaticsco.com

Burns Water Gardens
RR2, 2419 Van Luven Road
Baltimore, ON KOK 1CO
Tel: (905) 372-2737
Fax: (905) 372-8625
www.eagle.ca/-wtrgdn

Picov's Water Garden Centre
and Fisheries
380 Kingston Road East
Ajax, ON L1S 4S7
Tel: (905) 686-2151
Fax: (905) 686-2183
www.picovs.com

Water Arts Inc.
4158 Dundas Street West
Etoklcoke, ON M8X 1X3
Tel: (416) 239-5345
Fax: (416) 237-1098

AUSTRALIA

Classic Garden Products
18 Baretta Road
Wangara, WA 6065
Tel: (61) 8 9409 6101

Diamond Valley Garden Centre
170 Yan Yea Road
Plenty Vic 3090
Tel: (61) 3 9432 5113

Ponds & Pumps
6 Parkview Drive
Archerfield Qld 4107
Tel: (61) 7 3276 7666

Universal Rocks
39 Stanley Street
Peakhurst NSW 2210
Tel: (61) 2 9533 7400

Waterproofing Technologies
Level 1, 210 Homer Street
Earlwood, NSW 2206
Tel: (61) 2 9558 2161
Pond liners

INDEX

NOTES